JESUS · THE · IMAGINATION

The Passing of King Arthur, Julia Margaret Cameron, 1874

A JOURNAL OF
SPIRITUAL REVOLUTION

The Divine Feminine

VOLUME FIVE
2021

 Angelico Press

Published by
ANGELICO PRESS

Edited by
Michael Martin

Typesetting & Design by
James R. Wetmore

Send inquiries to:
Editorial Office
The Center for Sophiological Studies
Stella Matutina Farm
8780 Moeckel Road
Grass Lake, MI 49240
USA
mmartin@jesustheimagination.com
734-445-7327

ISBN 978-1-62138-717-6 pb

Front Cover: *The Empress*
Digital collage, Catrin Weltz-Stein

Back Cover: *Erupting Space*
Painting on canvas; acrylic and brass leaf
Stephane Gaulin-Brown

Cover Design: Michael Schrauzer

CONTENTS

Introduction: Leading Us Ever Onward

Michael Martin

Stella Matutina Farm
The Center for Sophiological Studies

"Let a body venture out of its shelter, expose itself in meaning beneath a veil of words. WORD FLESH. From one to the other, eternally, fragmented visions, metaphors of the invisible."[†]

JULIA KRISTEVA

 HAVE NEVER FELT COMfortable with Simone de Beauvoir's bristling in *The Second Sex* in regards to Goethe's concluding lines of *Faust:* "the Eternal Feminine leads us ever onward." De Beauvoir extends this complaint to allegorical representations of principles (like Liberty or the Church, for example) as female, to Dante's Beatrice, to divine figures such as the Virgin Mary and the Sophia of Gnosticism. De Beauvoir seems to operate under the assumption (note the term) that only feminine figures are idealized in Western culture, and that such are incommensurate with the actual reality of women. Idealization, however, is a universally human interpretive gesture; and that it is often personified can hardly be evidence of a conspiracy theory of male oppression, as if any man could live up to the model of Jesus, the Buddha, Odin All-Father, or even Pa Ingalls.

Figuration leads us ever onward, Simone.

Julia Kristeva, much more generous of spirit and, as a result, much more human, acknowledges the West's—and particularly Christianity's—psychic relationship to the feminine, especially as regards the image of the Mother. "The question is," she writes, "whether this was simply an appropriation of the Maternal by men and therefore, according to our working hypothesis, just a fantasy hiding the primary narcissism from view, or was it perhaps also a mechanism of enigmatic sublimation? This may have been masculine sublimation, assuming that for Freud imagining Leonardo—and even for Leonardo himself—taming the Maternal—or primary narcissistic—economy is a necessary precondition of artistic or literary achievement."[1] This notion can be applied, with some qualifications of course, to Goethe's pronouncement.

Goethe the poet, who was Goethe the scientist as well, however, was also giving utterance to a metaphysical

---

[1] Julia Kristeva, "Stabat Mater," trans. Arthur Goldhammer, *Poetics Today* 6, no. 1/2 *The Female Body in Western Culture: Semiotic Perspective* (1985); 133–52, at 134.

[1] Ibid., 135.

principle. Inspired by his reading of Boehme and the example of Novalis, an incipient Sophiology haunts the conclusion to Goethe's *Faust*. Many feminist commentators, like de Beauvoir, have chastised Goethe for not having Faust justly punished for his mistreatment of Gretchen—and the fact that Gretchen even prays for Faust's redemption from the heavenly realm during his apotheosis in the play's conclusion further offends them. But such a disposition profoundly misreads Goethe—and Christianity, for that matter. *Faust's* denouement is a picture of *apocatastasis*, the redemption of all, an idea that profoundly colors Sophiology.

What political discourses routinely miss when projecting their biases onto works of literature and metaphysics— to say nothing religion, science, or nature—is that not only the natural world, but the world of the spirit is also gendered. Try as we might, through whatever optics or interventions, we cannot ultimately avoid this reality. It is a matter of primal ontology.

Often sterilized in mistaken conceptions of neutrality, a gendered one-sidedness, as both Alison Milbank and Therese Schroeder-Sheker argue in this volume, is detrimental to everyone, regardless of gender. We act as though this is a reality we are only just now discovering—since the advent of feminism and ideas of gender equity—but this is not at all the case. It is my claim that the Western psyche has been clamoring for a regenerated imagination of the ontological reality of gender for at least a thousand years—and, as Margaret Barker discusses in my interview with her

here—the same Western psyche has been in search of a holistic and healthy imagination of gender from at least the time of Lady Wisdom's expulsion from worship in First Temple Judaism under the reforms of King Josiah.

During the Middle Ages, the Christian psyche was on the way to rectifying this situation. Beguine mysticism, with its holy feminine eroticism, Franciscan spirituality, with its deep relationship to Nature, and the lays of the Troubadours and their adoration of the Lady all rendered witness to the need of the re-entrance of the Divine Feminine into culture. That reformation was not to be fully realized, alas, though the dream lived on. Its palimpsest bleeds through Wolfram von Eschenbach's *Parzival*, in which the hero's development depends upon the counsel and examples of both women and men, even though he often misinterprets things at first. As we all do.

But perhaps the most accurate depiction of the phenomenon of which I speak in medieval literature is Sir Thomas Malory's *Morte Darthur*. The great medieval historian Jan Huizinga describes the late-medieval period in which Malory wrote as a time when "somber melancholy weighs on men's souls,"[2] and nowhere is this more evident than in Malory. Malory's Arthurian realm doesn't end in cataclysm so much as in dissipation and self-sabotage. As with Wolfram, women also figure in this story, but they also contribute to the ruin of the

[2] J. Huizinga, *The Waning of the Middle Ages: A Study in the Forms of Life, Thought and Art in France and the Netherlands in the XIVth and XVth Centuries* (St. Martin's Press, 1924), 22.

land and of chivalry. The knights who survive the Battle of Camlann, even the great Lancelot, end their lives as monks, priests, or hermits. Queen Guinevere herself dies in the cloister. A tremendous ennui taxed with apocalyptic sterility burdens both Malory's text and its readers. In the nineteenth century, Malory's melancholia reappeared in that of Tennyson, nowhere so strongly as in his *Idylls of the King*, a melancholic tableau brought to beautiful realization in the photography of Julia Margaret Cameron.

Malory is not entirely without hope (though what hope he offers is as delicate as frost), as Arthur does not die in the text. Malory tells us that in a mysterious bark "resceyved hym three ladyes with grete mournyng. And so they sette hem downe, and in one of their lappis kyng Arthure layd hys hede,"[3] and ferried him to the Isle of Avalon to be healed of his grievous wounds with the promise to one day return in parousaic triumph. Avalon is an island of women; it is only there where Arthur can find healing.

I have often thought, over this past, most melancholic of years, that Malory's tale is precisely the homeopathic medicine required for our particular moment. The West, and especially the Christian West, suffers from a grievous wound and it is only the Divine Feminine which can bring it healing. What was lost must be restored. In our end is our beginning. For the Divine Feminine leads us ever onward.

Holy Thursday 2021

---

[3] Thomas Malory, *Works*, ed. Eugene Vinaver, 2nd ed. (Oxford University Press, 1971), 716.

The Virgin, from the visions of
Anne Catherine Emmerich

CONIUNCTIO

Thomas Whittier

She didn't want to wake me, but staccato breaths call me across the threshold. Time for a bath. Time for the kettle to boil. It's warm for March, so we open the door. Robins sing and wrestle twine from garden stakes.

One March we made love in a pine grove. In the distance church bells pealed, while above us a family of crows sang like gypsies, invisible in the dark canopy. Though it was cold, we slept on the ground. Pine needles clung to our hair, and all through the day I could smell the pleasant musk of woman.

Tonight I will dream. I will dream I lift a stone and find the heart of a tree. Within, a mouse-colored owl sleeps in a nest of feathers. I will take two feathers before I leave, their quills weighted with flesh.

Oiling the Wheels of the Heavenly Chariot

Female Priesthood and the Divine Feminine

Alison Milbank

"She is the wheel within my wheel; her oil lubricates the wheels of my spirit. She lightens all my burdens. She makes all to blossom and become verdant, to laugh and rejoice. . . . O blessed Sophia! I confess that you are the most inward, hidden and invisible of spirits; that you are the quickest, finest, sharpest virtue and piercing energy, which penetrates my spirit and sensual and rational energies and capacities. . . . O divine Sophia, foster and perfect your work eternally! Work and weave inwardly with my wheels with your wine and oil, until you have utterly accomplished your work to your praise and glory!"[†]

JOHN PORDAGE

HILE SECRETLY AND silently, the divine Wisdom might be inspiring me and healing me with her wine and oil, I would not be quick to use such language in public worship in the modern Church of England, of which I am a priest. On the feast of Hildegard of Bingen, safe within the quire of a cathedral, such language might be appreciated, but although there is much stress laid on removing sexist language in liturgy and Bible translation, the divine feminine is neglected.

The debates which led to women being ordained to the threefold order of bishops, priests, and deacons were mainly conducted on the liberal terms of equality between the sexes. A key text to which proponents of women's ordination had recourse was Galatians 3:28: "There is neither Jew nor Greek, slave nor free, male nor female, for you are all one in Christ Jesus." If that were to be taken seriously, gender could not be any barrier to priesthood. Another argument for equality was the fact that from the beginning of the Church women were included among the baptized, along with slaves. Since believers put on Christ in baptism, this implies that any human baptized person can represent Christ, not just men who share his gender. There is nothing wrong with these arguments because, while they might accord with the secular agenda of sexual equality, they are theologically and biblically based.

[†] John Pordage, *Sophia*, trans. Alan G. Paddle (Minneapolis MN: Grailstone Press, 2017), 59.

Women have now been appointed to high office in the Church, but without any significant difference in the perception of God or change in the life of the Church, as had sometimes been predicted. Equality means in practice that women deans and bishops can be just as pompous or managerial as their male counterparts, and even as clerical. It has, however, led to the use of the New Revised Standard Version of the Bible in which gender specificity has been removed whenever possible, leading to some odd formulations, when a singular masculine is rendered by a neutral plural subject. Demands for equality have led to moves to remove gender from the divine completely, leading to dubious liturgical practices in which the Trinity is addressed as Creator, Redeemer, and Sanctifier or Liberator, suggesting that only one Person is involved in each activity rather than the whole Godhead. Furthermore, such phrases are implicitly modalist in reducing the Divine Persons to nothing more than roles.

While gender abandonment is smiled upon as progressive, sometimes the use of the feminine gender for the Holy Spirit is approved. There is some warrant in the tradition for this, especially as in Hebrew the word for spirit is female (*ruach*), although in Greek it is neuter (*pneuma*); Origen and other early Christian writers mention a lost Gospel to the Hebrews where the Holy Spirit is called "mother."[1] There is also an intriguing medieval fresco at Urschalling in Bavaria, which shows the Father and Son embracing what is presumed to be a young and female Holy Spirit. I am happy to use the feminine gender

for the Holy Spirit occasionally, but not exclusively, as there is no particular reason in revelation for a gendered Person. I sometimes feel that the feminine Holy Spirit is being presented to us purely in the service of maintaining divine gender equality.

Priesthood in the Catholic tradition had begun to place ever greater emphasis on the priest's representation of Christ in the Eucharist, forgetting that the presider is as much the representative of the body of Christ, the Church. This latter aspect has all but disappeared in ecclesial discourse and there is some resistance to the traditional use of the feminine to describe the Church as "she." As has already been established, all women priests may image Christ by virtue of their Baptism, and, in the same way, male priests can stand for the Church making the eucharistic offering; but visually the Church as the bride is particularly vivid when a woman presides at the Eucharist or Baptism. And it is there that the divine femininity begins to become visible; for this Church we embody is not primarily a fallible, human institution but a divine creation. The Russian theologian Sergei Bulgakov writes that "God created the world for the sake of the Church. That is as much as to say that it is at once the ground and goal of the world, its final cause and entelechy."[2] As a priest, it is my role to bring the world to its

---

[1] See Johannes von Oort, "The Holy Spirit as Feminine: Early Christian Testimonies and the Interpretation," *HTS Theological Studies* 72, 1 (2016) at http://dx.doi.org/10.4102/hts.v7211.3225, accessed 26/3/21.

[2] Sergei Bulgakov, *Sophia The Wisdom of God: An Outline of Sophiology* (New York: Lindisfarne Press, 1993), 134.

goal, the divine marriage, and as a priestess to image the bride in this union with Christ. As liturgical embodiment of the Church, women priests hold together the tension of the Church as an often-sinful institution with "the holy city, the New Jerusalem, coming down out of heaven from God, prepared as a bride adorned for her husband" (Rev. 21:2).

This role of Church is particularly meaningful for me personally when I celebrate the Eucharist facing eastwards, on the same side of the altar as the congregation and feel in solidarity with them. It is like interceding with a great army behind me, fulfilling George Herbert's description of prayer as "engine against th'Almighty."[3] It demonstrates that we are all together seeking the same goal, in contrast to westward facing, when the priest stands more in the role of Christ, like the host at the table, with the congregation on the other side. The eastward position reminds me of the cloak of the Virgin, sheltering the people of a town, the *Mater Misericordia* or *Schutzmantelmadonna* in German. Piero della Francesca painted a particularly hieratic version in Sansepolcro. The divine feminine is implicitly priestly in mediating between realities, just as women traditionally usher children into the world and care for the bodies of the dead.

Unlike most of my colleagues, I embrace the term "priestess," against which there are millennia of prejudices, ever since the male Jewish priesthood asserted itself against the polytheistic cults that had female priests, especially that of the Hittites, in which royal couples acted in priestly roles.[4] Yet if our physical embodiment has theological significance, a gendered understanding of priesthood seems wholly right, so long as we do not misuse it to fix women in particular subject positions. The image of God described in Genesis 1:27 is to be expressed in male and female, and suggests the complementarity of the sexes matters theologically, in a kind of *hieros gamos*. As Michael Martin points out in his introduction to *The Chymical Wedding,* it is "an ontological structure of the universe. In short: it's how things work."[5] St. Paul—or the person writing in his name—makes free use of this nuptial imagery in Ephesians 5, where husbands are to love their wives as Christ loved the Church. This language accords with the words of Christ himself about marriage in Matthew 19:5 where he teaches that the wedded man and woman become one flesh. As a way of imaging priesthood, the marriage analogy also restores the link between the priesthood of all believers and the ordained priesthood. For married lay people, the exchange of love and resulting offspring take on a sacred character as a sharing in the divine creation and restoration of the world, and for the single, their vocation becomes visible through a marital image as a commitment to the repair

---

[3] "Prayer," *George Herbert: The Complete English Poems*, ed. John Tobin (London: Penguin, 1991), 45.

[4] Ada Taggar-Cohen, *Hittite Priesthood* (Heidelberg: University of Heidelberg Press, 2006), 380–3.

[5] *The Chymical Wedding of Christian Rosenkreutz*, trans. Ezekiel Foxcroft, ed. and intro. Michael Martin (Kettering, OH: Angelico Press, 2019), 155.

of the world through work in a union with Christ rather than a human partner.

Outside of the circles of conservative evangelicalism on the one hand and conservative Catholicism on the other, which embraces its own version of nuptial theology, this language has become deeply problematic for the Church. In a world in which Judith Butler's concept of gender as performance rules, any idea of sexual difference is viewed as essentialist. The esoteric and alchemical traditions are helpful here because they emphasize both the nature of the coincidence of opposites—the chymical marriage— as a mystery and also the equal contribution of male and female elements to transformation. In modern feminist thought, the Belgian born theorist, Luce Irigaray, bears witness to this unknowability of gender polarity. She argues that due to patriarchal structures of thought the feminine remains unknowable and she seeks to establish a female imaginary to challenge and question this asymmetry. Since the feminine has been subsumed as a tool to allow masculine becoming, we just do not know what she might be. Irigaray calls for an ethics of sexual difference in which wonder, astonishment, and surprise may characterize relations between the sexes: "thus man and woman, woman and man, are always meeting for the first time because they cannot be substituted for the other."[6]

This restoration of wonder will, however, only be possible if a real sexual difference is restored to epistemology and women learn to understand their maternal genealogy. Only in this way will they have access to the divine, routinely imaged as masculine. What is important for Irigaray in imaging the divine for men and women is that the body and the material not be left behind. She even speaks of a "sensible transcendental" in which the break between physical and metaphysical is undone.[7] While Irigaray speaks of an angel as agent of mediation between the sexes, the winged figure that resonates with me and enables this theurgic return of matter is that of Holy Wisdom, who is often shown in the Russian icon tradition and also by Hildegard of Bingen as winged.[8] In Proverbs 8 she is a created entity but predates the making of the world. Her role is that of co-worker (in one iteration of the Hebrew as *amon*) or playful daughter (as *amun*); the ambiguity derives from the lack of vowels in written Hebrew, which allows either translation.[9] There is a further duality in the way in which a chiasmic structure of Proverbs 8:30–31 shows God

---

[6] Luce Irigaray, from *An Ethics of Sexual Difference* [1984], quoted in *French Feminists on Religion: A Reader*, ed. Morny Joy, Kathleen O'Grady and Judith L. Poxon (London: Routledge, 2002), 63.

[7] Luce Irigaray, *The Forgetting of Air in Martin Heidegger*, trans. Mary Beth Mader (Austin TX: University of Texas Press, 1999), 94.

[8] István Cselényi, *The Maternal Face of God: Explorations in Catholic Sophiology* (New York: Angelico Press, 2017), figures V, XIV and XV, 207, 216-17. Hildegard's is named as Divine Love in her writings but this figure acts exactly as Holy Wisdom.

[9] Peter Schäfer, *Mirror of his Beauty: Feminine Images of God from the Bible to the Early Kabbalah* (Princeton NJ: Princeton University Press, 2002), 26.

delighting in Wisdom, while she delights in his world:

> When he marked out the
>   foundations of the earth,
> then I was beside him, like a
>   master worker;
> and I was daily his delight,
>   rejoicing before him always,
> rejoicing in his inhabited world
>   and delighting in the
>   human race.

We see here some desire for divine immanence, which is expressed elsewhere in the Old Testament by the active participation of the natural world in the worship of God: the mountains skip like rams in Psalm 114.4 and the trees clap their hands in Isaiah 55:12. By the time of the Wisdom of Solomon, Wisdom has become "a pure emanation of the glory of the Almighty" and "a spotless mirror of the working of God" (Wisdom 7. 25–26). She is here the medium which receives and transmits God's energy and power. There are elements here of the Logos, as she is akin to the Nous in Platonism, imaging God's understanding and conveying it to humankind. And there are elements of the Holy Spirit since she is a breath who sanctifies: "in every generation she enters into holy souls and makes them friends of God and prophets" (Wisdom 7.27).

She seems to me a priestly figure who refreshes, renews, mediates, and reveals. The Rhineland abbess and mystical writer Hildegard had a vision of Wisdom as Divine Love, the energy that pervades the universe, and is particularly apt in envisioning the activity of the divine feminine. She writes in *The Book of Divine Works*:

> Thus I am concealed in things as fiery energy. They are ablaze through me, like the breath that ceaselessly enlivens the human being or like the wind-tossed flame in a fire. All these things live in their essence, and there is no death in them for I am life. I am also rationality, who holds the breath of the resonant word by which the whole of creation was created; and I have breathed life into everything, so that nothing by its nature may be mortal, for I am life.[10]

Faithfully following the Wisdom of Solomon, her figure combines aspects of Logos and Spirit, being Reason and the Divine Love and Power. She manifests the whole Godhead in some way, as is evident when one compares the visual representation of the vision, in which the fiery scarlet female figure holds the lamb of God, has the wings of the Spirit (and is in her whole fiery redness the Spirit as the bond of love between Father and Son) and is crowned with a male human head, representing the Father.[11]

Nothing closer to Sergei Bulgakov's conception of Wisdom as the divine *ousia* and the divine love could be imagined. "The nature of God (which is in fact Sophia) is a living and, there-

---

[10] Hildegard of Bingen, *The Book of Divine Works* I, I, in *Hildegard of Bingen: Selected Writings*, trans. and ed. Mark Atherton (London: Penguin, 2001), 172.

[11] An illuminated manuscript containing the theophany image, illustrating the first vision in *The Divine Works*, is in the Biblioteca Statale in Italy. The Lucca manuscript, as it is called, dates from 1230 and is a copy of Hildegard's own image of 1173.

fore, loving substance, ground, and principle."[12] Bulgakov's understanding of Sophia does the work that Irigaray asks for; that is, it reveals the transcendent as the source and ground of the immanent and shows that the latter "cannot exist without a *point d'appui* in the transcendent."[13] Womankind, so long associated with the material and earthly, is taken up into the Godhead but without losing her representation of the earth. In the words of Vladimir Solovyov: "Let it be known: today the Eternal Feminine in an incorruptible body is descending to Earth. In the unfading light of the new goddess Heaven has become one with the deeps."[14]

Divine Wisdom shows the priest her task. She must reach down to the lost and the forgotten, the abject and wounded and give them representation, shining the light of the divine love upon them, which reveals them as wholly lovable. The figure of Wisdom enables this fiery energy to oscillate between earth and heaven in order to reveal the holiness in matter and its origin in the divine life. Just as Adam and Eve were priests of God's creation in Eden, so the Christian priesthood needs to recover its creative potential. To quote Bulgakov again: "and when [God] had completed that work he entrusted human beings with all creation so that they could create with it in the same way that God created his work, that is, humanity."[15] That essentially priestly

act of blessing people, animals, and objects is not so much a consecrating of something secular or neutral or apart from God but an announcement of its origin in God and a proclamation of its holy source, to which it is reconnected. It is creative in the manner in which Adam and Eve named the beasts; that is, they did not invent, but discovered the creatures' true names through loving recognition. In a time of environmental crisis, we need to be priestly in relation to the whole cosmos and reveal the wisdom within animals, birds, and plants.

My own vocation to priesthood began when I became a mother. Lying in hospital, sharing in such a common human experience, I felt a new connection with other parents, and a sense of responsibility towards all children, as being as precious as my own. I would pray for them as I fed my little daughter in the middle of the night. Feeding and washing are natural daily mothering activities, and I do not forget their physical, universal basis in the ritual of the font and the altar, where they are honored and their divine basis established. Anointing the sick and the dying also has something of the tending to a child's grazed knee, or applying soothing cream.

As agent of Mother Church, I rely on the prayers and maternal example of the Blessed Mother, Our Lady St Mary. One reason why I value Bulgakov's sophiology is that it enables us to see Holy Wisdom active so widely, in the Trinity but also in Mary, the seat of wisdom. For me, Mary is a figure of female liberation, and the Virgin Birth a new creation, without

---

12 Bulgakov, *Sophia*, 35.
13 Ibid., 39.
14 Ibid., vii.
15 Ibid., 173.

male agency, and an empowerment of women. At the annunciation, God himself waits for the agreement of a teenaged girl to the incarnation and takes human nature from her. Her porosity to the overshadowing of the Holy Spirit is our model as priests. There was a minority tradition of regarding Mary as a priest in the early church and beyond. In a fifteenth-century oil painting by the Master of the Collins Hours, a giant Mary stands vested with the high priest's breastplate and a priestly stole as she feeds the faithful with holy bread from the altar, combining the shew-bread of the Temple and the Eucharistic host.[16] She is sometimes imaged wearing the pallium, a eucharistic stole sent to chosen primates and bishops by the pope.[17] Again, all priests, male and female alike, can copy Mary, but women priests can be her ikon, especially in the sacrament of Baptism, which is a particularly maternal sacrament, in which new Christians are brought to birth. Baptism is always carried out with flowing water, imaging the breaking of the waters in childbirth. The waters of chaos and death become a source of life, just as Christ in his maternal role opened his wounded side on the cross for an outpouring of new life in his water and blood. The fourteenth-century Norfolk anchoress Julian of Norwich speaks of Christ as struggling in labor on the cross to bring the Church

to birth. Therefore "our Lady is our mother in whom we are all enclosed and we are born from her in Christ; for she who is the mother of our Saviour is mother of all who will be saved in our Saviour. And our Saviour is our true mother in whom we are eternally born and by whom we shall always be enclosed."[18] As befits someone who chose life in an anchorhold, Julian loves these images of being enclosed and enfolded in womblike spaces. She has an extensive allegory of a servant falling in a dark hole, which represents variously sin but also the Virgin's womb, where Christ jumps in with Adam to save humanity. Such language enables the woman Christian to attain a symbolic imaginary, in which her body can image redemption and her maternal activity, bringing new Christians to birth, finds representation. And although Julian tends to associate Wisdom primarily with the Son, she has a suggestive passage which speaks of our essential being as a creation within the Godhead: "for the almighty truth of the Trinity is our father, he who made us and keeps us within him; and the deep wisdom of the Trinity is our mother, in whom we are all enclosed."[19] Perhaps Julian has in mind the *Mater Misericordiae* and her enveloping cloak? We have to remember also that in the ancient western marriage rite, the newly married couple were blessed under a great veil, which Julian will have witnessed many

---

[16] The painting is in the Louvre, Paris, entry 625.

[17] See Ally Kateusz, *Mary and Early Christian Women: Hidden Leadership* (Basingstoke: Palgrave Macmillan, 2019), 67–100.

[18] Julian of Norwich, *Revelations of Divine Love*, trans Elizabeth Spearing, intro. A.C. Spearing (London: Penguin, 1998), 136.

[19] Julian, *Revelations*, 130.

times.[20] This may also have been associated with the veil of the temple, which traditionally the young Mary helped to weave, as she wove the body of Christ. No longer does it divide sacred and profane but embraces us all in its folds, as we enter the body of Christ.

In this article I have suggested that women priests and women Christians generally need to visualize and embrace the divine feminine for their full participation in the divine life. I have argued that the mystery of sexual difference is an eschatological reality as well as part of the created order so that the marriage of Christ and his Church awaits full realization and the feminine symbolic needs to be truly established in a dynamic exchange of opposites with the masculine. We can find the feminine in the Blessed Virgin Mary, who gave life to Christ and above all in the figure of Divine Wisdom or Sophia, who undergirds everything and raises the material. For priesthood is a sign of the holiness of creation and a pointing to the heavenly wedding, the new heaven and earth. I quoted from Jacob Boehme's seventeenth-century clerical follower, John Pordage, in the quotation at the beginning of this article. He takes the wheel image from Boehme, and both

writers, like the kabbalists who share this figure in their understanding of the sefirot, from the vision of the divine chariot in Ezekiel 1. I chose this invocation of Sophia for its intimacy, for the strong sense of the Divine Wisdom as "a wheel within my wheel," but also as the lubricator of the spirit with her healing oil. When Anglican priests are ordained, they are anointed with the oil of chrism on their hands. This represents the gift of the Holy Spirit as in the hymn, *Veni Creator*, which is sung at the service. It addresses "the anointing Spirit" and asking him to "anoint and cheer our soiled face/ with the abundance of thy grace" as Bishop Cosin's translation has it.[21] There is an element of healing as well as consecration in Cosin's hymn and in Pordage's prayer. The physicality of oil speaks to the way in which the divine feminine heals the breach between matter and spirit, earth and heaven, immanence and transcendence. She is the gift of God to all humankind, but particularly to women, whose lived experience and particular association with the body and the material world has been misused to confine them. Through the holy oil her wheels can move and raise her through participation into the Godhead. For this oil is as inexhaustible as that of the widow's cruse in 1 Kings 17 or the oil in the temple lamp that was never extinguished. And with her wine, Wisdom delights us as we learn to share her own delight in the human race. In the Eucharist, the priest does not just offer bread and wine to the Father. She offers the body

---

[20] See the article by Henri de Villiers, "The Velatio Nuptialis: An Ancient (and Forgotten) Part of the Latin Marriage Rite" at https://sicutincensum.wordpress.com/2019/02/08/3006/ accessed 27/3/21. In some recent examples the veil of the bride is stretched out to cover the groom, even further emphasizing the divine feminine as shekinah or God's glory. Villiers even suggests that the Jewish wedding canopy may owe something to this Christian practice.

[21] It was first included in the 1662 *Book of Common Prayer* (London: SPCK, nd), 578.

of Christ, which is the Church, and in offering the Church the whole cosmos in its ecclesial destiny is included. Everything is given back to God to be blessed and revealed as connected to its divine source. And it returns to us divinized: Holy Wisdom is at work in that activity. I love the image of her as some heavenly mechanic, oiling the wheels of God's chariot. It is a particularly practical and humble image and one that we can embrace as priests, men and women alike, for it is God's people whom we serve and in whom his Wisdom dwells and with whom, with the whole created order, we shall rise in the divine chariot from glory to glory.

Olive Trees

ANADRAMOUS

Tyler DeLong

There is snow melt dripping
        along the eves
moved by the sun in the shifting of molecules
        solid and liquid
        in descent/dissent
        of the winter's grasp
but I long to hold on a little longer to the cold.

Warmth is nice I guess
but roofs leak in the thaw (this one doesn't, yet)
making wood swell
        and smell of dampness and must
warmth only worsening things growing mold
and breaking down fibers, weakening boards
which hold back the elements. We find shelter from weather
in the dwellings/thinkings we build
but never really escape ourselves.

I've heard You spoken of as a Mother bear
I find trees to hide in (but what are we?)
Your claws they do tear a man's chest
apart/plunging the depths of our
bones built like this shelter to escape Your seasons and Your weather
        whether or not we accept Your admittance (You break in all the same)
to the cavity we guard (right here, this sternum divided) and the dark cave
    you long to dwell in
You fill us, pulling sinew and stretching ligaments (we believe they hold us
    together).

Thistle and thorn, burr oak branches (see how they tangle, reaching as
    they do to the sky)
You leave no leaf unturned
bewildered, we draw near in the safety of Your hibernation (habitation)
only to startle at your stirring/waking in springtime
a Body which shudders and yet bears the weight of Eternity.
You are no man of haughty eyes and unclean lips
You weave as One with the stars
Vein-braider, You count the feathers of the sparrow and take an account
    of each scale
marking the coho in its run upstream.

I have heard you lay waste to our cities
and dispel the hunter's arrow
and that in a cloud of fire and smoke
You lead those who seek You into the wilderness.

Springs and Whirlpools

The Feminine Divine & the Undivine

Michael Sauter

"*DIVIDED FAMILY IS HELL. But there is something worse—a united family.*" This. It's not exactly a riddle, and it's different in tone than a typical, "muscular," Chesterton-style paradox, too, as it's decidedly more subtle. In breaking things down and opening things up at the same time, it works more with the force of flowing water than a battering ram. Note how it doesn't forcibly pry anything open for sociological analysis—"murdering to dissect"—but, instead, almost spring-like, (similar to the parables of Jesus), is itself alive and continues to bubble up, offering to the thirsty and crowded both refreshment and space. This *aperçu*, for me, has something so natural about it, almost like a Buddhist koan. And like nature, it is a bit "red in tooth and claw" while at the same time (again, like nature) has love smiling through it.

This perspicacious "family snapshot" is found in *Morning Light: The Spiritual Journal*, a little-known sophiological masterpiece written by French novelist Jean Sulivan, a writer whom Joseph Cunneen called "the most significant writer of Christian inspiration in France since George Bernanos." One of hundreds of such gems, the atmosphere of this book reminds one of the cave in Novalis's *Heinrich von Ofterdingen*: primordially earthy, but luminous with the precious stones which naturally stud the cave walls. Herein we're invited to ponder the mystery of family; both our natural human family and, by extension, the mystery of our Church family: *Mater Ecclesia*. And we are encouraged to take a mature, humorous, and sober assessment of the paradoxes of family, both its blessings and curses, light and shadows, in the hope that, in constantly freeing ourselves from any lies, decay, or bondage therein, we might stumble, as it were, into the mystery of the Kingdom/*Malkut*, (the central proclamation of the Gospels, and a term which, in the Aramaic of Jesus, is replete with feminine associations).

Corruptio Optima Pessima! In English, "the worst is the corruption of the best." Both painful and true, the mother who nurtures and sends forth can also, when not working from her best instincts, smother, devour and, Rapunzel-like, lock her children in a tower, keeping them infantile and making them weird. Parenting by helicopter creates children who are *loco*. The same is true for the family at large (men included, of course!). And also for "Mother Church." The Divine Feminine, in a sense, is made manifest to the degree that we can make peace with, and say *adieu* to the *undivine* feminine such that, in the words of Paul to the Romans, Creation may itself may be "liberated from its bondage to decay and brought into the freedom and glory of the children of God."

There is seminal importance found in the gestation of Sulivan's masterful book of reflections, which is really an extended meditation on these several faces of "Mother Church." "It had to be mother," he says, regarding the tune and tone (a spring?) he eventually discovered within himself and which, he understands, works as much "between the lines" of his writing as in the words on the page: "Let the almost nothing between the lines grow in you and take form." There is an atmosphere of spiritual freedom which emanates from these pages that compares with few others. The finished work, however, came only after years of intense struggle and rumination on the conditions surrounding the death of his own mother, a French peasant woman from Brittany who had the Gospels in her blood, but who, nonetheless and shockingly, suffered a horrifying "agony of abandonment" upon her deathbed. "Mother knew the Gospels by heart," he writes, "but had been indoctrinated by custom and the 'powers-that-be.'"

Two currents of faith, paraphrasing Goethe, lived within his mother's breast, and each "wrestled for mastery there." One had the bottom-up rhythm and revolutionary spirit of the parables, the Magnificat, and the Canticle of Canticles which reflected the variety, uniqueness, beauty, and naturalness of Mother Earth. This faith had, as it were, *inner* versions of the various waterways, footpaths, freshwater springs, and verdant greenery she saw around in the beautiful Breton countryside. It was alive and bubbled up like a spring. The other was the "Deposit" placed upon her, as it were, top-down, via a congested Interstate Highway System of concepts, obligations, and traditions, some with life in them but many others divorced from nature and (then and still) quite ossified. Comparing these two faiths is analogous to comparing "equal opportunity education" with "obligatory schooling," or "hospitality" with "hospitals." After time, and a certain amount of growth and power, all instances of top-down, clerical-caste encrusted, monopolistic institutions eventually muck up the springs that nourish them, and can even pervert and twist their missions, becoming whirlpools. Ivan Illich, a great observer of this process, called it "iatrogenesis," One example he studied as an analog to the process he saw solidifying in the Church was establishment medicine: "*The medical establishment has become a major threat to health*," he warned in 1974. It seemed shocking at the time, as if a nurturing institution could turn against its mission so totally; but here in 2021, as we enter the consolidation phase of the world itself is being turned into a large, totalizing pediatric ward with the cooperation of this same establishment, we might ponder a bit on the prescience of his insight!

Sounding an early and softer version of this same admonition 1600 years earlier, St. John Chrysostom warned, "Be careful of building hospitals as you will lose the virtue of hospitality." And the same process plays itself out in the schooling establishment, too, as novelist Stephen Vizincey noticed: "Strange as it may seem, no amount of learning can cure stupidity, and formal education positively fortifies it." Perhaps a similar watch-cry of sorts for the results of too much of a certain form of Church might be, "Too much Church establishment leads to the agony of spiritual abandonment!" Anyhow, Sulivan's mother experienced this iatrogenesis, the same blocking of the spring within herself. Shockingly, it even solicited her own cooperation, and her son took note:

> If some impulse prompted images and words that were sharp, she would blush at having let herself go. She undoubtedly accused herself of it in confession. There was only one humdrum road for her that led to Salvation, and it concerned only the hereafter. All questions had their answers as shallow as the questions. People were so attached to formulas justifying submission and pain that the formulas had become sacred.[1]

Sulivan's mother, like many of us, was a microcosm of Luke 11, "a house divided," and she followed that symbol's fateful trajectory. As she entered into the portal of death, her faith crumbled and she experienced complete desolation; her faith didn't "stand." Was Sulivan's mother a prophetic microcosm of the Church today? Sure, the wellspring and institution have always lived in tension, between Church as "it," we might say, and the Church as "She"—a tension more creative at some times than others. But it is possible that we have reached the iatrogenesis moment? This is where the spring doesn't just slow, but becomes twisted, evolves into a whirlpool and works disproportionately against its intended purpose. Upon his mother's tragic death, Sulivan underwent his own crisis of faith. For years he found himself in the condition of the Shulamite, a condition many of us have shared: "I went wandering through the city, through its streets and alleys. I looked for the one I love. I looked, but couldn't find him."

Lest anyone think what we have here is a familiar template for the beginning of a "I left the Church, and that has made all the difference" story, you're wrong. Yes, Sulivan's journey involves a trip East and time with Bede Griffiths, but all the more power to him for that! His was a journey to the depths, not a flight away to the shallows. As a Roman Catholic priest, Sulivan used his mother's experience in heroic fashion to take stock and come to terms with the same divide within himself. Like another Catholic priest, Ivan Illich, as well as the great "Fr." Francois Rabelais before them both, he didn't ever seek, or formally have, laicization imposed on him, but situations manifested through his courageous refusal not to follow his own version of Blake's "golden string" (a manifestation of the divine feminine *Shekinah*), such that, with this awakening, he was relieved from many of

[1] Jean Sulivan, *Morning Light: The Spiritual Journal of Jean Sulivan* (Paulist Press: New York, 1988), 35.

his formal priestly duties and exercised his priestly ministry in a new way.

> I GIVE you the end of a golden
>   string;
> Only wind it into a ball,
> It will lead you in at Heaven's gate,
> Built in Jerusalem's wall.

He found a new relationship with the divine feminine and, along with that, a new relationship with *Mater Ecclesia*. Submissive, locked-up and misshapen no more, Mother became for him, Wisdom and friend, and, in return, Wisdom entered his soul like a spring and shaped him into her own "friend and prophet."

As with the natural family, so with Mother Church; running away is one option, and often necessary at least for a while, but often (not always) leaves the escapee rootless, with more questions than answers, a prey to the latest ideologies peddled by the Corporate, State, and Science hucksters working on behalf of the principalities and the powers-that-be, (which are *all* versions of the fallen Sophia, Achamoth, of the Gnostics). This is the way of Homer's mythological multi-headed sea monster, Scylla: One gets rid of one demon only to welcome six (Homer) or seven (Luke 11:26) more in its place. These folk, even when they don't "officially" leave the Church, often end up even more sternly "religious," and, indeed, *possessed* by this secular religion, more so than the traditional pew-sitters, with creeds even more oppressive and proselytization more aggressive. Social justice, of course and no doubt, is central and comes out of a divine maternal impulse, but the type of unholy social justice that often evolves

here is the type characterized by our two diagnosticians of Church iatrogenesis as "institutionalized envy" (Illich) or the "reorganization of universal greed" (Sulivan), an undivine surrogate for the undivine Mother.

On the other hand, one can stay and remain insular while attempting to keep one's head above water as one treads along in the whirlpool, Homer's Charybdis (which is really an inverted, undivine spring). These unfortunates specialize in trafficking in "inside-baseball," Church jargon, and nostalgia ("nostalgia" being an infernal parody of the feminine, divine, nourishing and sap-like *Memorare*), and practicing pieties that, to the degree they've become arid and are not the result of a graced calling, are not much more than idols for OCDish mind-parasites and impulses. This is a return to the womb and, as a result, the "I" consciousness which is our calling eventually gets lost in the we-consciousness of childhood or the unconsciousness of the womb.

Special mention must be made here, in discussion of the undivine feminine, (at least in the Catholic world and in the West) of the peculiar institution known as seminary. Partaking of elements of undivine *Alma Mater* (school) in addition to *Mater Ecclesia* and, as of late (I write this during Covid-time and in the wake of the horrible sexual abuse scandal), existing under a new, informal, and unwritten "Civil Constitution of the Clergy," mostly forming not shepherds but sheepdogs for the totalizing State-become-Hospital-pediatric-ward, preaching social distance, Virtis, and "masks and vaccines as the greatest sign of love." With all of these undivine and disabling institutions wrapped up and stepping on each other and on seminarians, what we have here, as it is currently constituted, is something like "the unholy of unholies."

Seminary means "seed bed" and implies fructification, but, like a spring-become-whirlpool, what once may have been fertile ground has become extremely expensive, rocky, thorny, and biocide-saturated dirt. They need to be closed down. Instead of entering that vortex, those who are called to priesthood can take some classes, work manual labor for their keep, (preferably in real "seed beds"—at farms), live in community with the world, and pray. And, after they are ordained, they can also feel free, and be encouraged, to keep their hand on the plow or other day job. As it stands, instead of being trained in disciplines that reverse the spiritual order of the world, they become, in the words of Illich, "disabling professionals." Some break free from this disfiguring formation, but too many, disabled themselves by design and training, disable others like it's their job. Hurt people hurt people, as they say.

Jean Sulivan's mother had two currents of faith residing within her. Sadly, they existed in opposition. The answer, however, is not reducing the diversity of currents. No. All rivers and all traditions need more than one current. What is needed is currents that work in concordance/concurrence. The claim I am making here is that, through an individual's recognition and withdrawal from the undivine feminine, the Church doesn't become less feminine, but more so, and moves from the undivine to the divine. Concurrent with an ongoing

movement from the Age of Pisces to the Age of Aquarius, (the "water carrier"), and in a transition that can only be called radical, (in the sense of going back "to the roots"), another current will manifest and Wisdom will again build her house. Valentin Tomberg described this "alternating" current, *ever ancient ever new*, as "a revelation of Sophia, present as a heart revelation in the mother of Jesus":

> Along with the revelation of the prophets there had always existed another current of Revelation; this was the current of heart revelation of the mothers and grandmothers of the expected Messiah. The Messiah was not promised only prophetically, but was also discerningly loved and lovingly discerned in the silent depths of the heart. Nor was this a dim discernment; it was a wordless, silent cognition. This does not mean, however, that it was vague or uncertain. Although a great clarity and certainty may exist in the heart's discernment, there may nevertheless be no organ to express it in words. Such wordless unspoken discernment lived for many centuries alongside the cognition spoken by the prophets. Indeed side-by-side with the written book of the Old Testament we must consider another, unwritten book—one containing the wordless revelation of the heart of Sophia. A radiant comprehension of this invisible book lived in the heart of Mary.[2]

[2] Valentin Tomberg, *Christ and Sophia: Anthroposophic Mediations* (SteinerBooks: Great Barrington, MA. 2011), 142.

Getting this current flowing again is akin to the mission and result of getting a spring unstuck, which is a common theme and occurrence at Mary's apparition in La Salette France (1846) and many other Marian apparitions in our own time. I can personally testify that this alternate current, if faintly, trickles still in the silence and "pious mumbling" at the Cistercian Abbey where I work, and its song is present, too, in many practices of popular piety such as pilgrimages and novenas. In the "Age of the Show" (all foreground), this song is difficult to hear, and this is by design as, like Mary's Magnificat, it's the most subversive and revolutionary force known to man and the Principalities see it as a threat. In the words of the Emerald Tablet of Hermes, and like water, She "is the strongest of all powers, the force of all forces, for it overcometh every subtle thing and doth penetrate every solid substance." She is in the background, and exists between the lines on the page and reveals Herself in the contemplation of matter and in the sounds of a bubbling of a brook. Listen. Listen well.

THE COLOURS OF ATHENS

John Milbank

Stones to float
for the
redeeming of rock.

Solid to veiling
dissolves
what it fully reveals
into waving voluptuousness.

Weight is borne away
in youth.
The full light
of *kores* and *dike*
carried over
and aerially afterwards.

With parade and patience
of devouring glory.

Reality upswept
in surplus of motion.
We catch its spume
and it does not sting us.
Nor ever could,
we sense immediately.

The eyes garnished
with the elements
they pixelate.
A dominion of ochre
mediating flame
to crimson victory.
Blue merely the
prelude to a blur that is
swelling and thunderous.

The missing green
of time
is after all the cosmos.
Athena chose
the olive branch
and consigned water
to destiny.

For a rhythmic
human surging
like a wave
passing along itself.
The reined-back reigning.

Meander balances
stasis and flow
to fringe all liturgy.

There are white cubes,
narrow poplars
and flanking planes
that can no longer
offer much shelter
for espionage.

The temple to red forging
is an open kennel,
a pointless cage
whose bars cannot contain
the fearful power
to shape but also to wrench
it would entice here.

But beached
from the upper sea
basks lightly above
the serene shrine
of ever-floating
Wisdom who
yet seeks the lost city
she once inaugurated.

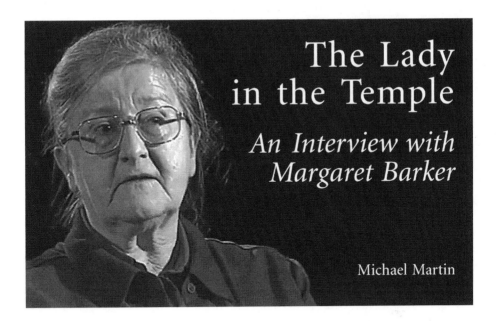

The Lady in the Temple

An Interview with Margaret Barker

Michael Martin

iBLICAL SCHOLAR, THEOLOGIAN, METHODIST PREACHER, MOTHER, and grandmother Margaret Barker has forged a new way of doing scholarship and theology outside of the often claustrophobic walls of academia. Her facility in the ancient languages and amazing gift for connecting the threads of liturgy, history, and scripture have resulted in some of the most momentous discoveries of at least the past century, starting with her first book, *The Older Testament*, in 1987. Her subsequent excavations—in *Temple Theology* (2004); *The Hidden Tradition of the Kingdom of God* (2007); and *The Mother of the Lord, Volume One: The Lady in the Temple* (2012), to name only three—have resulted in some of the most startling insights into Judeo-Christian history, not least among them concerning the figure she calls "The Great Lady." Not only does Barker's work impact biblical studies, but her discoveries also bring renewed hope and theological justification for an integral Christian understanding of the Creation and thereby of ecology (quite accurately in Barker's hands, "a logos of the dwelling place") as put forth in her book, *Creation: The Biblical Vision for the Environment* (2009).

I was unaware of Barker's work when I began writing *The Submerged Reality* in 2014. My background is in poetry and literary studies, so my entrance into the mystery of Sophia (Barker's Great Lady) was by way of English seventeenth-century poetry, religious writing, hermeticism, and mysticism. When I discovered Barker's *The Mother of the Lord, Volume One* shortly after finishing *The Heavenly Country*, I grew tremendously excited. Here, I realized, was even more evidence that what Boehme, the Philadelphians, Robert Fludd, Solovyov, Bulgakov, Florensky—the great sophiologists of history—had discovered possessed not only personal, mystical relevance, but could also boast a pedigree grounded in the biblical revelation, albeit obscured through subtle redactions, political intrigues, and the mists of time. I simply had to interview her. Below is a transcript of our conversation, one that was interrupted by plenty of laughter.

MM: Margaret, what was the "aha!" moment when you discovered the reality (as you have framed it) of First Temple Judaism, particularly as regards the presence of the Lady in the Temple?

MB: Well, I have been blessed with a whole series of these moments, I have to say; and anyone who reads my books will realize where I have had them. I think the first one was when I was preparing to write *The Great Angel*, which was published in 1992. I started off writing exactly the opposite book, and I realized just how much evidence I was having to throw away. I took a decision to abandon the book I had planned and write a book using all of the rejected evidence. That was a very big "aha!" moment, because I realized that rejecting evidence that doesn't fit your theory is actually rather a very bad scholarly habit—but a lot of people haven't recognized this. So my first big "aha!" moment was realizing the whole story of the second God in the Old Testament and all the things that found a great problem— like why do texts that apply to Yahweh in the Old Testament get applied to Jesus and all this kind of stuff. It's no problem at all. The problem is the creation of modern scholarship's presuppositions. And you have to "whack" the text to amend it and so forth in order to explain why it doesn't fit with what you wanted to say. But if you go

with the text—and I *hate* that expression people use, "controlling your sources"—I always say "I don't control my sources; I let them control me." And that produces radically different results. And that was my first one.

My second "aha!" moment was when I was present for the first time— this would have been in the late nineties—at a liturgy of the Orthodox Church. I was staying with friends at Oxford and they were Orthodox. They said, "Oh, come with us to church," and I did. I was watching this (then) strange ritual—all the movements of it—and I was following it. The bishop presiding, a lovely man, recognized this stranger in his midst; and he came to me afterwards and said, "This all must have been very strange for you." And I said, "On the contrary. I recognized every bit of it." His eyes went out on stalks (we've been good friends ever since, I have to say). I sent him Temple texts and so forth that were relevant to what I had just heard; and he sent me a whole lot more evidence for what I was doing. I've still got it—it's all highlighted in yellow pen. That's when I realized where my Temple studies had gone— and that they had survived intact.

Then I had a whole series of these things. One of them was when I realized for the first time that the fundamental image used for interpreting the death and resurrection of Jesus was not Passover, but the Day of

Atonement, and that "Christ our Passover is sacrificed for us"—St. Paul's famous verse—was, in fact, a fingerpost pointing you up a cul-de-sac. What you really needed to do was look at the book of Hebrews, particularly chapter nine—which is not brought in as often as it should be. There, of course, is another great piece of the Temple. So that was another one: reinterpreting the old atonement material in terms of the Day of Atonement. It was about this time that the Church of England's report by Doctrine Commission called "The Mystery of Salvation" came to no conclusion at all about atonement—which is a very Anglican thing to do. No conclusion at all—but they didn't mention the Day of Atonement! This seemed to me the most extraordinary piece of evidence selection, if you like.

Then, more and more, I've grown to appreciate the material that's encoded in icons—traditional styles of icons. Only eighteen months ago when I was in Israel in a church, looking at the icons. I suddenly realized that a pair of icons of Mary were, in fact, representing the two major aspects of the Great Lady of the Jerusalem Temple three-thousand years ago. It's things like that. You can't explain them. You just look at the links and say, "Well, this can't be coincidence." This certainly isn't the product of a university research group looking for interesting things to join up. It's something that has come through.

And, so, I have been blessed with a lot of these "aha!" moments; and each one produces a great burst of writing—in some cases changing what I'd written twenty or thirty years ago. Which is why it annoys me when some people write or email me and say, "In 1985 you said this, this, and this, and now you contradict yourself." And I think, "Well of course you do!" That's how your thought grows.

MM: I agree. Some academics will get their diploma and often feel obligated to the person they were at that time—and never really grow or change. That's not how it is.

I've always been intrigued by the Wisdom books, especially the so-called Apocrypha, a fascination which I recall starting as a boy in Catholic school when I found out the books aren't included in the Protestant canon of scripture. They still fascinate me—questions about their authorship, the language in which they were written, the community or communities in diaspora in North Africa in which appeared, and their exclusion from the canon of the Hebrew Bible. What is their role in the story of First Temple Judaism?

MB: The Wisdom books in the Hebrew scriptures that we have at the moment, as far as I can see, are quite carefully sanitized versions of something that had once been a major intellectual strand—if not the dominant strand—in Temple theology. Because of what it was and what it represented—mysteries, the heavenly aspect, the angels, all those smells and bells things—a lot of it has been excised; and so the texts that we have in the canon—which I use to define Wisdom texts (or they were used to define them) are not actually representative of the genre as it was. Scholars like putting labels on things, and then having boxes you can put things in. There was a box labeled "Wisdom," and a box labeled "Apocalyptic," and another box labeled "Prophecy." And then people started discussing the relationship between them, when, in fact, they're all the same thing, but just different aspects of it. It is interesting that the received, you know, proper history of the Old Testament times that we learn in college and so forth when we're very young has no mention of the people we read in the Old Testament as the prophets. This is a question that usually passes without comment. How is it possible to write a history of Israel, Judah, Jerusalem— I'm thinking of Samuel and Kings primarily—how is it possible to write about all these great events and not mention Amos and Hosea? (Well, Isaiah gets a walk-on part—he's the doctor who visits the king and prescribes him a fig poultice).[1] You would never believe that this two-line cameo appearance of Isaiah—the greatest thinker of the First Temple—and he's simply not there! And so you say, well, how representative is the collection of Hebrew books we now have as the Old Testament, the Hebrew scriptures?

Then you have, of course, the Wisdom texts, so-called. It used to be thought, round some rather loose and lazy thinking, that the Wisdom texts were not included in the Hebrew canon because they weren't originally written in the holy language of Hebrew. So that was the reason to exclude them. And then the great book of the Wisdom of Jesus Ben Sirach has now been found in Hebrew—

now, not all of it, and the text isn't quite the same as the Greek one (odd words here and there); but, basically, it's the same. So we know that's not the reason they were excluded. When you whittle down all the other reasons that have been offered, you realize that the reason they were excluded is that they represented something that mainstream—I won't say mainstream Judaism, but the people who controlled the formation of the Hebrew canon—did not like them and did not wish people to read about them. The themes in those books are not of wisdom as a philosophical concept, but Wisdom as a divine being. And because this divine being has so many names, I always call her the Great Lady—a capital G and a capital L— and then introduce her titles later. But it's clear from the way that the Great Lady passes into acclamations for Mary that there is a direct link. I was brought up as a good Protestant girl and I was taught that, "Oh, well, it's those Catholics looking around, grasping for any straw to put to their Mary stuff"—it's simply not true! There is a direct link from the titles of the Great Lady, Wisdom, as she appears in the so-called apocryphal books and Mary; and you can trace them. This was another of my "aha" moments. I was talking to an Orthodox friend—a very learned Orthodox friend—and telling him about some of the titles I had discovered for the Great Lady of the Temple. He just stood up and pulled off a well-thumbed book from one of his shelves and said, "Do you know this?" It was an edition of the Akathistos Hymn to the Mary (obviously in Greek). I didn't know at the time. I looked

---

[1] 2 Kings 20.

through it. He told me what it was. And since then I have gone back again and again and again—I can now identify all but, I think, three of the titles of acclamation in that great liturgical poem; I can source them all to the Great Lady of the Temple going back to the time of Isaiah. Again, that cannot have been the product of a hymn-writing research group. That was a living tradition. And we've got to trace these streams through. I just wish we could recruit more Catholics, particularly, who've got a—what's the word I want?—a kind of "cradle-given sense" of Mary and who could spot this better than I could. I'm very much a visitor to this area. I can do the scholarly stuff and say, "Oh, look, there's one of those, and one of those, and one of those"—but I don't really, because of my upbringing and background, have an instinctive feel for it. That's something you do have to grow up with.

With the Wisdom literature, we have to bewail the fact that there are no capital letters in Hebrew. Wherever we find "wisdom" it's assumed to be, like in Psalm 104—"With wisdom you have made them all"—that it's the Creator who was just having a good idea at the time. But if there had been capital letters, we would have known what we find in Proverbs chapter eight that the Great Lady, with her title "Wisdom," is Co-Creator. That raises all sorts of amazing questions. We look at things like the Story of Creation in Genesis chapter two, where Adam is formed from dust. What is it that makes the dust coagulate into clay? Well, it's something that the Authorized version translates as "mist," but it's actually a Hebrew word that we don't know what it means.

The Greek translates it as "the fountain." And this fountain—which was later used as a title for Mary—was the fountain that allowed the dust to coagulate into a human being. And there's some lovely theology for you. Absolutely beautiful. You have to read this curiously cryptic material—and try and read *with* it rather than hover over it with a scholarly glass and say, "Yes, here we have a varied reading." And all the other stuff that we try to do. You need to approach very much with the imagination and sympathy.

So the Wisdom texts are the way forward. The interesting thing about the Wisdom texts is that they don't have any "Chosen People" stuff; they don't have any sacred history and killing-all-our-enemies stuff; and they have a huge amount about seeing the hand of the Lord in Creation, the patterns in Creation: learning to live within Creation and learning from it. It's not pantheism. It's just common sense, actually. As we are now realizing. So I do hope that the environment movement takes on more of the Wisdom teaching—not just in sentimental sense. Very often when that happens the texts are taken out of context and it's very embarrassing to listen to them.

MM: (laughs)

MB: Well, it is! "Consider the lilies of the field, how they grow" is not about looking at wildflowers on verdurous motorways. It means a different thing completely. But if the environmentalist or Creation theology people could embrace Wisdom a bit more—and stop calling it "the environment"! Call it "Creation." That would be the first stand to make. Then, I think, the importance of the Wisdom tradition and also how it came to be excluded—and what replaced it: that would be a very interesting learning exercise for all the churches.

MM: That's inspiring. In addition to being a scholar, I'm also a biodynamic farmer. So that speaks to me.

But it's interesting—your mention of not having grown up with a Marian spirituality. My scholarship is mostly concerned with sixteenth- and seventeenth-century religious texts, particularly in England, and a number of Protestant mystics—Jane Lead and the Philadelphian Society, for example, and Jacob Boehme—and how they rediscovered Wisdom. They also didn't grow up in the atmosphere of Marian spirituality. Your work, in a similar way, recapitulates that on another level: a rediscovery of Wisdom.

Your work is decidedly revolutionary, certainly ground-breaking; and I think its implications are far-reaching, touching not only academic theology but also challenging received understandings of what Judaism and Christianity *are* at their foundations. So how do you see your role and the role of your work in the landscape of contemporary Christianity?

MB: Oh, that's an impossible question to answer. I don't actually sit and contemplate my role.

MM: (laughs)

MB: I actually get on with the job. And if the contemporary thinkers and so forth don't like what I do, well,

that's absolutely fine. They can go on doing what they like doing. People sometimes say to me, "Why do you not quote your contemporaries?" And I say, "Whom do you suggest?" Because, of course, if you're doing something totally different you're not going to find a lot of cross-referencing in the secondary literature. Now, I use the primary sources; and I try always to start with primary sources—and not primary sources in translation. Translating is a very interesting activity and can totally skew the meaning of the text. I would cite here some so-called "modern" and "easy-to-read" Bible translations, which really border on the blasphemous. And how people can read from these things, and then say, "This is the Word of the Lord," you know, may they be forgiven.

MM: (laughs)

MB: Absolutely horrendous. One of the criticisms that I sometimes face is "Why do you always use your own translations?" To which I reply, "Why do you think?" Implicit in the question, of course, is the answer. I don't think of my work as being revolutionary. I don't sit and contemplate, thinking "Where am I?" I sit at my desk and I pursue threads where they go. I have a network of wonderful email contacts who write to me with marvelous ideas ("Have you come across so-and-so?"). To which I write back, "No, but thank you." So I have an unofficial network of, well, not research assistants, because they're co-fellow-workers, if you like. But few of them are in the halls of official academe. Most of this work is going on outside of universities. A lot of it is going on with clergy who have a pastoral charge, and consequently they have very little time. But the real work in this area is not—and I'm making a big generalization here—is not being done in universities. I look around, and I think, "Well, it would be nice to plant this in universities." But then I look around and I think, "Well, where amongst all these departments with, you know, tenured staff, is there a mix of people with expertises that would be able to pursue this?" And the answer is, "Not at all" because you need twenty, twenty-five, thirty years to change the staffing profile of a department, if there's tenure. By that time, some people will be dead.

MM: Absolutely.

MB: Absolutely. So we're stuck with what we've got—and they have possession of the family silver.

MM: (laughs) That's true.

MB: I've spent some time in academia, I'm still kind of tangentially involved; but that's not where innovation happens.

MM: It is certainly not. One thing that has always puzzled me about the religious streams of late antiquity is what I take to be a kind of appropriation of Wisdom (Sophia) by various Gnostic currents, where in some respects she figures as something of a cosmic screw-up, an archetypal problem child. I wonder if this mythos somehow echoes or is a palimpsest of the Alexandrian Jewish community's veneration of Wisdom. What can you say about the Gnostic Sophia in relation

to that community (or communities) and First Temple Judaism?

MB: Oh, yes. Indeed. This is one of my favorite things, where I can get up on my soapbox. If you take as your starting position, as I have as my premise, that the world, religion, theology of the First Temple was very different from the Second Temple, you then say that the source of so much of the "non-canonical tradition" is the First Temple. From the First Temple there arose, obviously, Christianity. Pythagoras was influenced by the First Temple; you can see in his official golden biography[2] says he spent some time in and learned the secrets of the temple in Syria—I'm not quoting precisely there, but that's the gist of it. I have worked and published a little on this, but I have worked a great deal at showing how the earliest authentic— the nearest we can get to the authentic sayings of Pythagoras—are actually drawn directly from the priestly teaching of the First Temple. And, of course, that's what the ancient people said: you know, that Pythagoras learned from Moses or some such thing. And modern scholars in their wisdom say, "Oh, they would say that, wouldn't they?" They dismiss it.

MM: (laughs)

MB: Well, it's true! It's so silly. Because even the very late-medieval and Renaissance kabbalists would tell you that kabbalah—which is another thing from the First Temple—that kabbalah and Pythagoreanism are the same thing...and Christianity.

[2] *The Golden Verses.*

Gnosticism is one of the many children of the First Temple. If you look for Wisdom in some of the Gnostic texts (you can't put all the Gnostic texts in the same basket, by the way)—again, I don't want to get into the heresy of putting them in different boxes, because then they don't meet each other, But I think what you need to look for there is the tracing of claims to be the teachings of Seth, going back to Adam, his father. Now, there's a lot of so-called "Sethian Gnostic texts." If you look at those, you remember that "Adam" was the name for the first High Priest in the Temple tradition; and so every high priest was the "Adam." Adam got chucked out of his Eden temple. We know when that happened; that was about 597-586 BC, His sons were the "People of Seth." If you look particularly at the Sethian texts, make that your starting point, it's very easy to see. If you take the Coptic names, for example, the Coptic concepts, and say this was taken down as dictation by somebody whose Hebrew was not terribly well-articulated, you can see behind those garbled Coptic names the structure of First Temple theology. The parallel to the Great Lady is not Sophia, but it's the being who appears in these texts as Barbelo. If you look at how she is described in the Sethian texts, and you look at how she is described under the title "The Living One" in the visions of Ezekiel (chapters one and chapters eight to ten) you can see that there's absolutely no question. It's like putting two blurred photographs next to each other—but you can see they're the same person. So you can gain a lot from looking at—I suppose you can't make a special

study of garbled Coptic, but that is what it actually involves. The Gnostics are pre-Christian, but they have a great affinity with Christianity, simply because they are the children (or grandchildren, if you like) of the Great Lady of the First Temple. So there is an affinity between Pythagoreanism and then, particularly through the *Timaeus,* into Platonism. Then there was that happy accident of history that the Neoplatonists in Syria, when they were having their big revival, set up their headquarters right down the road from where the Temple mystics were living in exile—and I don't believe they didn't meet each other. So you can see where those sort of cross-fertilized. And we've had a lot of overeager identifying of labels, always assuming that Christianity was somehow derived from the dreadful foreign things. Whereas, in fact, they are all co-heirs, if you like, of the First Temple. We really do need to rejig that template. It's not been helped by the fact that Classical paradigms were set up by scholars who had usually studied the Classics to a high degree before moving secondarily into Semitic languages, or Coptic, or whatever it might be. That is now changing, but paradigms with which we were brought up—and which still people cling to as if it were fact, rather than theory—assumed that the Semitic sources were somehow inferior to the great men of Athens and all the rest of it. Whereas, if you just look at the dates, it's quite clear that Ezekiel was an awful lot earlier than Plato. And yet he's using the same vocabulary. There's a lot of tidying up to do.

MM: Finally, how has your scholarship, this amazing and fruitful journey, changed or impacted your own religious sensibilities or spirituality?

MB: Well, I think first of all it's made me realize that the Protestantism in which I was brought up—which was very much Bible-based and had the great merit of insuring that I knew my Bible and could quote great tracts of Isaiah and Psalms—that was absolutely good. But what was bad was the *sola scriptura*, scripture alone, and that has been a huge impediment to the progress of scholarship. That is fading now, but that certainly influenced the giants on whose shoulders we stand. One of my big changes, of course, is moving away from that background whilst acknowledging it did give me a very, very good working knowledge of scripture that is very important. I find that when I'm working with people from other traditions that they have very flimsy knowledge of the canonical texts. On the other hand, they can bring to the discussion a greater sense, if you like, of liturgy and the sacred and things like that. So we have to learn from each other. I often say that you can trace my journey from the fact when I was a little girl in Sunday school I used to give my Sunday school pennies, my collection, to convert Catholics.

MM: (laughs)

MB: And now, of course, I regularly speak at the Shrine of the Lady of Walsingham. They've heard that story many times, but that in itself tells you what you need to know. The Lord has a sense of humor, and it gets us there

in the end. But I've also found—I've been a Methodist preacher now for many, many years, since 1984—I have found that preaching in this way and from this base, that people are very receptive. There's no such thing as an "ordinary congregation," but you know what I mean. You turn up on a Sunday morning and you have your allotted twenty minutes—and people are really interested. You get comments like, "We never heard that." The one that has been the biggest change for me was a different way of preaching Good Friday. Once I had switched from the Passover Lamb to the Atonement sacrifice—and what the Temple means by "atonement"—which is *not* "penal substitution." That is something that has *got* to be removed from our preaching. It is absolutely immoral, and, you know, those who continue in this way will answer for it. That's something that has changed dramatically for me. A lot of our hymns, even our modern hymns, are really singing either a lot of nonsense or a lot of things that one couldn't possibly preach from the pulpit. But they have catchy tunes and people think the words must be right.

MM: (laughs)

MB: And that's terrible, absolutely terrible. I have grown, obviously we all do, we change. I think deep-down the criterion I bring to my research is no use in my preaching. It's no use. They don't get lectures from the pulpit—that's obviously a different type of communication—but even in a homeopathic dilution it does affect the way you interpret texts, the way you explain texts . . . a little bit of background you weave in. Like that. I think that's important, because I think if the business of biblical studies is divorced from the teaching function within the Christian community you've got to ask yourself a very big question about the relevance of that form of biblical study. A lot of the stuff that's really fashionable—and I go to conferences and listen to this stuff dutifully—and I think to myself, "Would I ever use that from the pulpit?" And the answer is "No." If you are trying to sell a product that nobody's going to use, your business is not going to flourish. And if these business were not subsidized heavily by inherited wealth and State backing, all this kind of stuff—I think of the great institutions, like my own in Cambridge—they could never survive in the marketplace. Not the big faculties—some of the more niche faculties. You do say to yourself, "Well, if it's for the preservation of ancient knowledge and all that other stuff, that's fine, but some of the modern stuff that's being done—this, I think, flimsy and ephemeral stuff that has spun off it and decked out in fancy language in order to distance themselves from the plebs who don't understand this 'real scholarship…'" That makes me just so angry. These are people in a privileged position who, frankly, are not using it properly.

MM: I'm in total agreement.

MB: What can we do? The system is

what it is. And so, I said earlier, the people who are making real progress in this area—and I could probably tell you of fifty worldwide who are in my network, they'll all have their networks—they're all outside academe. One of the questions I sometimes put to people who say, "Well, you know, you must have objectivity in all this"… I say, "If you had someone who was a Professor of French, who didn't speak the language, who had never been to France—and doubted if the place even existed—would you take him seriously?"

MM: (laughs)

MB: And the answer is, of course, "No." Or, "If you had a medical school, none of whose graduates were fit to practice medicine, and none of whose research related to the human body—what would you do?" This is the situation we're in. And you become very unpopular for saying it. But, on the other hand, someone has to say it. It's such a shame. It's not that this work doesn't exist. It's there. But the question is getting it out to the consumers. Our little Temple group does study days in parishes—which is fine—but six hours once a year isn't going to start the revolution.

NATURE IS BEAUTY IN ALL HER FACES

Daniel Nicholas

Nature is beauty in all her faces:
Dry bark, thornscrub, and bloodied beak
Are ikons of a sinless homeostasis,
Obedient subjects of a law that seeks
To keep her good and mine entangled
(the living breath free and unstrangled),
To unscroll its script in each gull and grub:
That even the cockroach is coaxed by love;
While the grotesque is got of our own invention,
In the meonic misery of the imago dei,
Whose unrest the world would soon unsay
If not for Nature's good intention.
For love must grow, be it unsafe to roam,
That beauty might beckon her children home.

Woman at Loom, Edwin Holgate

Knee-Woman at Loom

Therese Schroeder-Sheker

Letter Home

RDAINED MINISTERS OF all ranks (cardinals, bishops, priests, deacons) can be referred to as clergy, yet bishops and cardinals in the Roman Catholic Church shoulder unique authority and institutional shaping power. Some clergy serve as papal consultants—merely advising—while others have voting power. The two words *clergy* and *clericalism* sound similar but differ greatly. In speaking about the systemic institutional dysfunction known as *clericalism*,[1] Pope Francis condemns the abuse of power and the abuse of conscience. Modeling what has been called a language of "disorienting inclusivity," Francis states in his August 20, 2018 "Letter to the People of God" that clericalism tends to "diminish and undervalue" and "helps to perpetuate many of the evils that we are condemning today." He emphasizes that "these wounds never

disappear," and uses the strongest possible terms: *crime, atrocity, betrayal*. He repeats himself using an imperative: "*emphatically say no to all forms of clericalism.*" Last but not least, in this letter, Francis rises above gender discrimination by using the words "all" and "any" when referring to the People of God; the "people" is all of us and entails no contingency. With that inclusivity, he begins and ends his letter by weaving the feminine into his exhortation. Discover Mary's song, Mary's immeasurable gift, capacity, and model if we want to involve ourselves in "ecclesial and social change." This is what he says.

Mary's feminine *charism* stands in marked contrast to the clericalism the pope is condemning. While all the apostles except one ran away in fear and confusion, and went into hiding, Mary remained to witness everything, as did the two other Marys. Though agonizing, Mary the Mother and the youngest apostle, John, stood together, merely feet away from the Cross, remaining fully present to Jesus. That is how and why (then and now) they radiate the love preached and lived by the example of the Master. Their model illumines moral and spiritual authority in a way that is timeless and above reproach. Their courage and love were woven together seamlessly, in equal parts, as were

---

[1] The Association of US Catholic Priests, June 2019: "Clericalism permeates the entire structure of the Church, separating lay people from the clergy, ordinary clergy from the bishops, and all of us from the many-layered Vatican bureaucracy" and "creates a façade behind which serious systemic problems are minimized, hidden, and sometimes completely denied. Clericalism corrupts and frustrates what the Risen Christ and the Holy Spirit intend for the Church of our time."

both feminine and masculine *charisms.*

That inclusion of the feminine in Pope Francis's letter seemed promising, inspiring. Perhaps a sea change? To my sorrow, finding coherence between it and the operational aspects of the institution remains challenging. Catholic theologians, historians, sociologists and others have identified and explored multiple issues arising from the gendered and hierarchical structure of the Church. Rosemary Radford Reuther, Elizabeth Schüssler Fiorenza, Sandra M Schneiders, and many others[2] have painstakingly explored the struggles of the post-Vatican II Church. As priestly associations began to emerge, publications reflected the priestly voice in new and sensitive ways. Eventually, scholarship began to annotate the untenable dilemmas wreaked for both priests and laity via intractable institutional clericalism.[3] It wasn't until the media addressed the scandals of sexual predation and administrative obstruction that the enormity of the affliction began to be understood in the pews.

From 1970 to 2020, most of these fundamental issues as well as a cascade of related ones had already been identified and addressed in research of considerable acuity. However, formal studies offer in-depth analysis, presenting their works in tomes and academic journals, and sometimes in privately commissioned reports, never

made public. Since many of these publications were unknown to a majority of worshippers, or perhaps inaccessible to them, the media *exposé* of the mechanism of the scandals has had a devastating impact.

One of the germane issues dislodged in this climate returns to the structure of the institution. The crisis addresses the lack of inclusivity demonstrated in a church structure that claims a membership of one point three billion persons globally, but distances itself from half, or six-hundred and fifty million of them. These are *the other half* of Ecclesia, those waiting in the antehall. Women work in positions of responsibility in parishes, hospitals, universities, and law firms, but cannot participate in Rome in the way that the 227 cardinals and 5582 bishops[4] might because they are female rather than male. Thus, the barrier.

Cynthia Stewart[5] says "While the Church's hierarchy remains entirely male, a strong majority of Catholics participating in lay ministry are women. In fact, about eighty-five percent of all church roles that do not require ordination are held by women. The Church developing out of Vatican II began allowing women to take on liturgical roles such as readers and Eucharistic ministers, girls as altar servers, and admitting women to degree programs in theology. Suddenly, women were theologians and

---

[2] Bibliographic references available in the forthcoming book *Knee-Woman at Loom.*
[3] William Doherty, PhD's masterful "Priestly Celibacy and the Rise of National Priests' Associations since Vatican II." Marian University, May 9, 2018.

[4] Data on clergy, the Curia, institutes and religious orders is published at Catholic-Hierarchy.org.
[5] Cynthia Stewart, PhD. The *Catholic Church* (Anselm Academic, 2008).

parish administrators, professors teaching Catholic history and doctrine, experts in canon law and liturgy, and many leadership roles."

In February of this year, the French Sister Nathalie Becquart was appointed as an under-secretary to the Vatican's Synod of Bishops office. This has attracted many headlines and a few presumptions about a voting position, but whether or not she will be invited to vote on anything is unclear. Reporters do not always understand that even bishop's synods serve and consult. The Church is not a democracy.

Ethicist/theologian John Dalla Costa[6] says that flesh-and-blood Catholic women "*are at the apogee of being ignored.*" Theologians of many schools of thought question an elite fraternity that excludes women from deliberative or leadership processes and a hierarchy that is inadvertently suspicious of the feminine dimension wherever and however it is lived.

From a pastoral point of view, the clericalist *attitude* is unsupportable. It wounds because it disenfranchises human beings. It renders inconvenient people, events, or conditions invisible or mute; excludes rather than incorporates; condemns rather than welcomes; upholds double standards[7] or hypocritical positions; weaponizes sacraments; stresses legalism over grace. Clericalism is not the whole story, but it is a noisy one. During a

recent quiet talk, one of the physicians with whom I work closely posed a question to me of devastating sincerity: "*If Jesus walked the Earth today, would He even recognize this Church as the one He founded?*" I have been gulping ever since that burning moment.

Many describe the *feminine* as capacity, dimension, and reality, and I particularly favor understanding it as a capacity, a way of being. As such, either woman or man can integrate this *charism* into selfhood; yet, without its integration, a human being is developmentally arrested.[8] (The same is true in reverse for women; without healthy integration of the masculine, they too remain afflicted). In 1972, a study commissioned by the United States Conference of Catholic Bishops

---

[6] John Dalla Costa's article on "Restoring the Church's Moral Authority" is published in *With One Accord*, vol 1, Winter 2020, by the Magdala Colloquy in Toronto.

[7] See the history of automatic excommunication (*latae sententiae*).

[8] American bishops commissioned psychologist and former priest Eugene C Kennedy (1928–2015) to ascertain the psychological health of priests. His landmark study, co-authored by Victor J. Heckler, "The Catholic Priest in the United States: Investigations," found only 7 percent of priests were "emotionally developed," another 18 percent were "developing," 66 percent were "underdeveloped," and 8 percent were "maldeveloped." Hopefully, Kennedy's research helped draw attention to ways in which maturity could be supported in the future. On ACP (Association of Catholic Priests) Fr. Brendan O'Rourke, a Redemptorist priest, speaks beautifully: "The journey from the false self to the real self may be part of the journey towards maturity for many priests, moving from a service of (rather impersonal) duty, to one of genuine care, compassion, and justice. Unless priests work at being in relationship with themselves and others their ministry will suffer. The Word of God needs to resonate in their whole selves. They need to preach with their whole selves. They don't need to be perfect but they do need to be real."

found that two-thirds of the priests who participated in the study lacked emotional maturity and had been unable to achieve healthy, trusting, and non-sexual relationships.

Can we find even a single person, profession, or vocation that doesn't manifest some proclivity towards an internalized and patterned flaw? Professions as a point of maturity and professionalism subject themselves to rigorous internal critique in order to foster self-knowledge and make continual improvements, but they do not function within a structure like the Church. Their members have agency. So the question arises: how can the one point three billion be with this predicament? What is a caring response, a wisdom response (as opposed to a condemning attitude or an enabling posture)? To that end, I return not only to the feminine as *charism* and human capacity but to understanding the mechanisms that prevent growth. What prevents the integration of all that makes one whole?

Many see the feminine *charism* as relatedness and inter-relatedness; however, the *armamentarium* of clericalism is structurally reliant upon the opposite: distance and distancing. *Set apart* and *set above*. This is how the Washington priest[9] and lawyer Fr. Peter Daly describes the priesthood; he has the advantage of being able to speak from within commitment, as opposed to a heckler speaking from a noisy highway. He says that priestly formation can unwittingly re-enforce notions of superiority, setting seminarians apart and above. Regardless of intent, the clericalist or distancing patterns which rely upon separation dismiss and marginalize people and events while giving the distanced a false sense of importance. In doing so, clericalism works to ensure the internal disconnect from selfhood as well as from Ecclesia.

With an adjustment, something like a fine-tuning or a change of key, clericalism could abandon the tendency to flee or fear. It could enlarge its hearth in order to cultivate understanding and trust. In suppressing either the feminine dimension or the *vox feminae*, clericalism widens the internal gap and hinders its own potential. Where oh where does this leave Wisdom?

It seems to me that any gap impairs the weaving of a truly Ecclesial fabric. After all, we *are* Ecclesia, and clerical self-harm does as much harm to the fabric of the Church as it does to the feminine dimension at large. Do not these kinds of rips also scourge the mystical body of Christ?

Following Vatican II (1962–1965) and again during the last two decades following the 2002 *Boston Globe* exposé, the Church has suffered successive waves of exodus. Many describe that they have made the paradoxical choice to walk away *in order to remain faithful.*[10] Henri de Lubac

---

[9] Fr. Peter Daly, "Tackle Clericalism First When Attempting Priesthood Reform," in August 13, 2019 issue of *National Catholic Reporter.* His ideal is priesthood *reform* (in contrast to James Carroll's call to abolish the priesthood).

[10] James Carroll's cover article for June 2019 *The Atlantic* as well as the rebuttal authored by Robert Sirico.

describes paradox[11] as *"the search or wait for synthesis. It is the provisional expression of a view which remains incomplete, but whose orientation is ever towards fulness."* Equally courageous, many hover in liminality, betwixt and between, close to home yet still in a form of exile, remaining *in the pews* as "restless pilgrims," struggling over matters of conscience.

The fourth-century monk Evagrius[12] taught the faithful to place their heads on Christ's heart, an intimate posture of seeking, listening, *praying* and *trusting* the source. (Another Evagrian proverb: *If you are a theologian, you truly pray. If you truly pray, you are a theologian.*) The monk's examples are distinctly different from an impersonal experience of the disconnect that is endemic because of *scale.* Each Christian can imagine with the fullness of their strength, love and awe a personal relationship with Christ. The scale amplifies the potential. Remember Schumacher's *Small is Beautiful: Economics as if People Mattered*? Being one of over a billion souls navigating a large structure managed by a relative few (who are very far away) amplifies loss of scale. Likewise, being one of the six-hundred and fifty million women relegated to the waiting room in silence amplifies loss of scale. The losses are disheartening, and sometimes beyond human com-

prehension. We can, however, choose to attend to intimacy with Christ, lest we ourselves aid a withering, desiccating way of being.

> *"The total submission of the spirit to Revelation is a fertilizing submission, because it is submission to Mystery. But the total submission of the spirit to any human system whatever is a sterilizing submission."*   ~ Henri de Lubac[13]

Other than being clear, the various pilgrims—priests, nuns, sisters, and laity—describe that they do not always know what to do or how to be with that which is morally untenable in the institution. How to hold it? The Benedictine Sister Joan Chittister[14] has elaborated her commitment exquisitely, calling her decision to remain *in the pews* as "a ministry of irritation." The Church she loves so dearly, she says, "needs women for its own salvation." Sister Joan gracefully accepts being a thorn in a bunkered side and in so doing, she is aiding millions. James Carroll is emphatic that the power structure of clericalism is *"not* the Church. The Church is the people of God. I refuse to let a predator priest or a complicit bishop rip my faith from me." Any number of priestly and lay groups continue to grapple and struggle over contentious

---

[11] Henri de Lubac, *Paradoxes of Faith* (Ignatius Press, 1987). Also, "The real paradoxes suppose an antimony: one truth upsets us, another truth balances it."

[12] Evagrius Ponticus (345–399) *Ad Monachos*, trans. and commentary Jeremy Driscoll (Newman Press, 2003). Also, John Eudes Bamberger's edition of *The Praktikos: Chapters on Prayer* (Cistercian Publications, 1981).

[13] The various de Lubac quotes that serve as banners throughout this recital are from his *Paradoxes of Faith* (Ignatius Press, 1987) and *More Paradoxes* (Ignatius Press, 2002).

[14] Sr. Joan Chittister identifies herself as a "restless pilgrim" in her June 14, 2020 issue of *Vision and Viewpoint.* This issue is excerpted from her "Why I Stay," in *From the Writings of Joan Chittister: On Women* (Benetvision, 2020).

issues; they raise profound questions while listening to His heart.

Sadly, we have another historical event that has far-reaching consequences. Pope John Paul II's decision to contain the issues raised by the many capped further discussion. Clericalism imposed formidable control on the narrative and its emissaries sometimes rebuked[15] the articulate voices of associations and individuals. Some chapters of this historical tension appear (to me) more with the quality of a duel rather than a dialogue.

"For lack of a mirror, you cannot see your face. For lack of adversaries, you do not know your failings."
~Buddhist monk Nichiren[16]

A reflexively defensive position (or a reflexive denial) says more about abject fear than it does about the earnest pilgrim who is crying out to be heard and received. The Jesuit Fr. Jim McDermott[17] expresses the systemic problem of hypocrisy with heartbreaking candor and healing insight. "We clergy can become caustic where we're meant to be caring. We build walls when we're supposed to be vulnerable. We live in hiding while we preach 'Be not afraid.'" With a compassion that moves me deeply, he addresses institutional terror in a way that every human being can understand:

Overwhelmed by the boundless wilderness that is the human heart, they grasp at ways to feel in control. And so they insist on definitions that don't match lived experience, scientific study or the example of Jesus. These are not the acts of individuals trying to embody the endlessly welcoming love of God, or even just trying to be a source of goodness in the world. They're the choices of people who find themselves out of their depth, angry and afraid.

Aren't many of us also out of our depth at least some of the time? Sadly, fear extends its tendrils like a vast underground mycelium and none of us are immune. However tragic the view, this preamble offers one window into missed opportunities. Throughout centuries, the institution has missed the opportunity to learn *in new and living ways.*[18] This affliction and set of symptoms is also why a peerless and beautiful feminine figure appeared to Hildegard[19] in 1170 saying *"the foxes have their lairs, the birds of the sky their nests, but I have no helper or consoler."* With the eye of the spirit, Hildegard sees that Wisdom has no place to rest. Ecclesia has no place to rest. The exclusion of the feminine wisdom-capacity for relatedness is an institutional pattern with mileage. The princes of the Church have a place, and the whole of Creation has a place, but not I, she says, in tatters. Not I. There is no place for me. This is heartbreaking.

And so it is that historians and sociologists (William Doherty and Dean Hoge) firmly document an institutional crisis that has afflicted vast

---

[15] Robert Sirico, *The Atlantic*, June 2019.
[16] Henri de Lubac, *Paradoxes of Faith.*
[17] Fr. Jim McDermott, "A Place for Us," *National Catholic Reporter*, March 5, 2021.

[18] Hebrews 10:20.
[19] Peter Dronke, *Women Writers of the Middle Ages* (Cambridge University Press, 1984).

swaths of the population globally. So then, how shall healing be supported?

"In the order of the spirit, a method of painless birth will never be found."
~ Henri de Lubac[20]

It seems to me that all Catholics, regardless of their exact temperature, constellate the warp and weft of a divine cloth. Like it or not, consciously or unconsciously, each person in Ecclesia reflects almost two millennia of the sacraments, depth, glory, mystery, creativity, beauty, holiness, prayer, sacrifice, insight. The opposite is also true. Each person in Ecclesia reflects every error ever made, including almost two millennia of institutional gaps, punctures and rips lodged by lop-sided and opaque imbalance rather than transparent inclusivity.

Since Catholicism is being tattered with each successive rending, isn't it crucial to return to the loom to begin to repair, restore, and renew this sacramental fabric? Garment, raiment, vestment, or tattered rag. *Which shall it be?*

It seems to me that the quality of a newly emergent cloth depends upon at least three phenomena: 1) the re-awakening of conscience; 2) the

[20] Henri de Lubac, *Paradoxes of Faith.*

renewal of intelligence-of -the-heart; and 3) the complete and total adoption of the *disarmament* with which Jesus lived his life and fulfilled his mission. Disarmament, not the arsenal of *armamentarium.*

These three can be integrated by virtue of the presence of both *charisms,* the feminine and the masculine, together, if we choose to banish tokenism and inhabit holy proportion. We could experience polyphony at its best if the *charisms* are woven together in a single harmonious voice. Echoing the wisdom of Schumacher's subtitle, it would be Church as if people mattered. It would be Church as if relationship with the People of God in the pews *mattered.* The new music could ensoul the entire community of women and men *and* circulate as choral epiphany. This sonic bridge can make the fabric of Ecclesia audible and whole again. Will any of us live to see it happen? Some days the institutional headlines are more dismal than others, but the good news is that I don't really know many who are throwing out the baby with the bathwater. In the same way that a candle lit in the darkness always renews a sense of awe, many faithful are doing what that 4th century monk suggested so long ago as the deepest source of prayer and theology: attending to intimacy with Christ.

Knee-Woman at Loom

Traditionally, skillful crofters had a miniature form of weaving called darning. Few may remember how to darn today, but our grandparents and ancestors still knew this skill. When

the sun set, after a day's work was done, a crofter on the island of North Uist or Mull would sit near the light of the hearth and darn. This happened during a few moments of tranquility, when the only sound might have been the crackling of the burning wood on the fire, the snoring of a nodding loved one sitting nearby, or the rustling of the wind against a windowpane. The crofter darned the ripped or threadbare heel, toe, or elbow of the woolen sock or jumper. There was no inclination to discard the entire garment because of the rip. This darning was a way of honoring the previous effort required to shear, wash, card, and spin the fleece, and to knit the original garment from the gift of the creature. It was also the way one honored the lamb whose wool kept each man, woman, and child on the island warm. The material substances and the skilled labor were recognized, lauded, unified, and conserved. In the islander culture, ecology[21] and holiness were related even if the word ecology was not on their tongue. Creatures and Creator were connected and reconnected, nature and humanity were connected, and the moments of weaving together the threads literally brought *relatedness* into the fore, right into the rhythm of daily life.

No, I am not nostalgic about a preindustrial past, but I do value the wisdom embedded in traditional solutions to perennial fissures and disruptions. In an era in which the public trust of institutions and systems has been eroded, as have ours in the post-truth era and the year of the pandemic, we might emphasize darning as a metaphor.

"Those who obtain something without trouble keep it without love."
~ Henri de Lubac[22]

Though much of Scotland today is Presbyterian, there was a moment in the sixteen-hundreds when three great Hebridean *sennachies* related the following[23] about their Catholic community, because they had received "evil news":

> *"Every person in the Western Isles—by order of the King by and with the advice of the Parliament— young and old, male and female, was to be murdered. Their soil and their land, their inherited personal wealth were to be given to the murderer."*

After a time they met again on Black Ridge. *"There was great pathos in the meeting. Would they be cut with an axe or strangled with a cord?"*

They related how they hid a few books and parchments. To fortify themselves, a few days later, each stood on a rock and took an oath. They vowed:

> *"to preserve inviolate their history; to pass it on reliantly by means of instruction, from mouth to mouth, from knee to knee, the testament and the heritage most precious in the power of the free, in opposition to the unfree, without injury to any person or any thing, without distortion of the truth in opposing deceit, without strengthening evil, without*

---

[21] Hyun-Chul Cho, S.J. "Interconnectedness and Intrinsic Value as Ecological Principles: Karl Rahner's Evolutionary Christology," *Theological Studies*, 70 (2009).

[22] Henri de Lubac, *Paradoxes*.
[23] Editors Donald A Fergusson, Aonaghus Iain MacDhomhnuill and Jean Gillespe London, *From the Farthest Hebrides* (Macmillan, 1978).

weakening justice, so long as the blood is warm, breath in body, to the awakening of the Feinn."

This same vow their *sennachie* descendants continued to make until 1916.

Later, one of the women survivors said: *"It is not what is written that teaches, but what is remembered."* The only reason I relate this electrifying moment is to dispel any notion people might have of my romanticizing a crofter's life on a wind-swept island. In painting the picture of their (disarmed) response to violent persecution, it is another way of describing how deeply and authentically the islanders were tested in their faith and for their faith. *Without distortion of the truth in opposing deceit* is a commitment from which we could learn worlds again today. They seemed to have achieved an ensouled embodiment that was infused with the Holy Spirit. How else could anyone face an axe?

So, from my perspective, in turning to the Scottish district of the Hebridean Islands, the weaving together of thread, proverb, prayer, and song emphasizes the feminine dimension in new and living ways and shows how others have bridged the structural distances that have been historically divisive.

I would like to return to an insight from von Balthasar[24] on the French Jesuit Henri de Lubac. The former is highlighting essential differences between *decentralization* and *democratization*; he notes how de Lubac describes the dangers of an "anony-

mous bureaucratism." Again, we encounter the loss of scale and loss of intimacy that discloses the source or mechanism of so much damage. To continue with von Balthasar: "Here the fundamental thesis is that ecclesial authority can only preserve its necessary character of 'fatherhood' (instead of institution) where the 'motherhood' of the Church is recognized and affirmed as the enveloping medium."

To the extent that any form of clericalism unwittingly requires fealty to forms of cognitive dissonance today, we *enable* the retrograde movements which are infantilizing rather than ripening. To the extent that the Church trusts and cherishes more richly than it once controlled or condemned, it invites us to walk with Him, to follow His example. Could this evocation of the crofter's disarmed wisdom intimate something of the New Jerusalem? And, in it, a potentizing future? I stand trembling because I am certain that freedom is a heavy mantle, can include staggering responsibility, and freedom is never to be confused with cheap license. It is the opposite. I am also sure that an Ecclesial fabric in tatters, with broken strands frayed and splayed, is no mantle at all. Darning—imagination and practice—might help us remain connected despite the grave temptation to walk away.

People often say: *the Holy Spirit works in mysterious ways.* For millennia, the Holy Spirit has been associated with the feminine for some theologians and mystics, though certainly not by all, and the *magisterium* prefers to render the Holy Spirit with a masculine pronoun. Perhaps we are asked to go behind the scenes in order

---

[24] Hans Urs von Balthasar, *The Theology of Henri de Lubac* (Communio Books, 1991).

to remember the Holy Spirit in action. Hans Urs von Balthasar's Sophianic insight once described Mary and John together as a *disappearing center.* These two words provide a golden key about the nature of transmission and authority. Power and strength are not the same. One uses force, and the other is disarmed. However buried, submerged, exiled, or ignored the feminine dimension has been in the structure of an institutional Christianity, we can receive at least some of the most vital signs, signatures, footprints, and patterns expressed in her wise voice if we look to exceedingly rich conditions that anthropologists identify as *anti-structure.* Not anarchy: *anti-structure.* No bunkering. The silos are deadening. *Only love is credible,* von Balthasar says.

For these many reasons, when I consider the divine feminine, I have turned to the traditional artisanal handcrafting cultures of the Scottish Hebrides to enter the heart of the matter. The missing half (the feminine dimension as capacity and *charism*) can be witnessed in the wisdom of islander artistry, which is always a demonstration of radical receptivity. This island culture was deeply connected to Nature, brought to birth all of its artisanal handcrafts in recognizing, honoring, and incorporating the organic fruits of Creation into their crafts. This is so because the crafts entailed the wisdom needed for survival. They weren't the expressions of frivolous uses of precious resources. Artisanal handcrafts worked only with locally gathered fruits of the earth. Nothing was wasted; much was made of seemingly little precisely because cleansed sight embodied their *ability*

to recognize and cherish Creature, Creation, and Creator unified in coherence. This coherence lets a culture of disconnect fade or dissolve. It lifts a culture of direct contact. Is this a leap? Or a fact? It is my impression that it is both.

The unabashed mastery of beautiful speech and artistic handcraft (expressed by each crofter) recovers "the missing half" so lost in the structure of the continental church institutions. It was not something anyone set out to "do" as a resistance movement or a reform movement. Their artisanal handcrafts *were* life because they included and required the engagement of every man, woman, and child on the island, co-operating together, with local substance and local creatures. Karl Rahner highlights this ecological holiness, in contrast to a dualism that separates. All art is inherently subversive and potentially spiritual, but something exceptionally true, good, and beautiful once happened on North Uist, Skye, Mull, Heisgeir and Iona for a brief corridor of time because of their ecological wisdom. I attempt to learn as much as possible from this legacy.

Living on only a few square miles and being exposed to the thunderous waves on all sides, islanders were surrounded by and immersed in the continually changing elements of nature. Wind, wave, current, mist, and cloud shaped consciousness and work. Constantly changing light, rhythmically pounding surf, ephemeral cloud formations, and shimmering horizon lines ensouled the fabric of elemental relationships. These continually presented the crofter with the visual glyph of a living streaming process of metamorphosis. Unlike a citizen living in vast, cobble-stoned, or cement-laden cities on the mainland or continent such as Edinburgh, London, Paris, Madrid, or even in the medieval cathedral towns of Melrose, Chartres, Florence, Aachen, or Canterbury, there was no place, time, cottage, or croft in which an islander was isolated or distanced from the process of metamorphosis expressed in the environment. It was continually manifesting itself in nature and unfolded right in front each person. On little islands sometimes only a few square miles, and within one-story cottages, no architecture blocked view. This glyph was equally available to all.

I am convinced that these audible, visual, fragrant, and tactile shaping forces supported, galvanized, and purified a different kind of life, one of embodied clarity, ensouled speech, and spirit-infused consciousness. Together, these three created an egalitarian culture of modesty and practicality. In this way, a truly catholic Sophianic Wisdom was once alive and well for more than a hundred years. That is why I want to "go there" as a meditation on the divine feminine.

Time and contemplative *praxis* have taught me that *loom* is to memory as *altar* is to ritual. Those who are inheritors and practitioners of both traditions (weaving and prayer) recognize that each of these worlds is inclusive of rhythm, breath, sound, substance, and vision. Until as recently as the nineteenth century, *loom* and *altar* were perceived as natural companions for those living throughout the Hebridean Islands.

Veritable streams of song, prayer, poem, proverb, myth, and essential traditional handcrafting activities fructified and amplified one another while enhancing every dimension of island life. A pre-industrial life in the Western Isles was decidedly rugged, and yet reflected the holism of an early and distinctly local form of Christianity. This attunement allowed the complete life cycle from birth to death and the practical (material) survival skills of the islanders to be steered by thoughtful and prayerful reflection. Disembodied abstraction had no home in this heritage.

Daily life and labor were so thoroughly permeated by silent, whispered, spoken, sung, and crooned prayer that the daily performance of crofting labor combined with the skilled artisanal handcrafts practiced everywhere in the archipelago manifested something like an islander's *divine office*.

Their lives were rooted in a *lived* and embodied sense of Scripture, highlighting intimate relationships with Christ, Mary, saints and angels, many of whom were evoked hourly. Their prayers name and laud the details of Christ in Nature and Christ as Lord of the elements, Christ in billowing clouds, or Mary[25] brighter than the waxing moon, Mary the fragrant, Mary as the root of gladness. Meditative prayers were woven into the fabric of life, and this kind of praying took place wherever work activities were taking place. *"I went sunways round my dwelling, in the name of Mary Mother."* Though at

[25] Alexander Carmichael, *Carmina Gadelica*, vol. 1.

times a largely Catholic population, these ways of praying could occur in private solitude and sometimes be echoed in small circles.

The praying while working did not require clerical mediation but rather it affirmed the recollected presence-of-being of whomever was active with the work at hand, or leading the work at hand, regardless of gender. An example of this was found in the midwifery activity which included not only the delivery of the newborn baby but immediate baptism, right there at the bedside. The mid-wife was known as the knee-woman. The priest would and could perform a second baptism later.

The many Hebridean arts mentioned above were richly developed, inter-connected, faithfully transmitted, and insightfully preserved in *oral tradition*. The example of the sennachie vow quoted earlier is a perfect example of the seriousness of the commitment to preserve their own traditions. The sennachie memory was legendary in capacity, holding generations of history, ritual, prayer, song, and proverb by heart, not to be confused with the endearing banter two or three shared over a pint of ale. Only in the twentieth century (as islander population dwindled) did their traditional ways of knowing finally begin to appear in the written form, first in mystical literature,[26] and

later in scholarly[27] ethnography and various academic disciplines in the humanities and soft sciences. More recently, documentary series have aired on television, and small paperback anthologies of Gaelic blessings abound, though the prayers are presented out of context.

Both traditions, *oral* and *written*, indicate how interior relationships such as *loom* and *altar* once freely intersected for islanders, all of whom were still directly anchored in and personally connected to the crofter's life. Their perceptions of meaning were not contingent upon university credentials or religious sanctions, but rather engagement, direct contact, *praxis*, and devotion. Relationship between such frameworks as loom and altar "showed up" inwardly as a result of three dimensions of life: the metabolization processes implicit in deeply meditative and rhythmical artisanal handcrafting activities; the ensouled quality of the prayer life; and, finally, in what the islanders called "the living tablet of memory." The content of this memory was a cherished, supple fabric, something woven of multiple strands, all local, not syncretic.

This memory seems to have been alive and streaming, as something shared by individuals and communities. The fabric existed for the good of one and all and did not resemble or

---

[26] Works attributed pseudonymously to Fiona Macleod: *The Divine Adventure: Iona; By Sundown Shores: Studies in Spiritual History* (Chapman and Hall, 1900); *The Winged Destiny: Studies in the Spiritual History of the Gael,* (Chapman and Hall, 1904); *Where the Forest Murmurs: Nature Essays* (Charles Scribner, 1906); etc.

[27] See Margaret Fay Shaw, *Folksongs & Folklore of South Uist* (Oxford University Press, 1977). See Donald A. Fergusson, *From the Farthest Hebrides*. See Alexander Carmichael's five-volumed *Carmina Gadelica*, edited by Angus Matheson (Scottish Academic Press, 1928). These 5 volumes differ greatly from the popular pocketbook anthologies.

even attempt to replicate the university, laboratory, or religious content associated with the modern copyright, trademark, or *imprimatur.*

Oral tradition is thus a wisdom-vessel that germinates, ripens, blossoms, moves, and circulates itself. In weighing prayer, proverb, song, and story, one can see it move in arcs, lemniscates and spirals. We can see it gradually precipitating in stages from vision (imagination and inspiration) to tangible materiality. The intelligence of *oral tradition* moves naturally, not unlike respiratory cycles. It descends from the spiritual and metaphysical, to the stirrings of the intelligence-of-the-heart, and descends right down to the hands, limbs, feet. It becomes physical, embodied, generative, life-supporting, and life-ensuring as demonstrated in the visible fruits of artisanal labor.

What is it that is so powerful about a few square miles of remote, wind-swept earth, often treeless, always rocky, seeming dots and patches of land surrounded on all sides by the pounding of wave and the cry of the seal? What role did environment play in nurturing and protecting the forms of culture and authority in which the islanders flourished? What is it about the particular islander consciousness reflected in their wisdom and crafting that is so startling today?

Separated from large cities by wild seas and powerful elements, one might be tempted to assume a population stranded in formidable paucity; yet, instead, we encounter riches: prodigious creativity, quiet authority, subtle intelligence, and impressive self-reliance. Their heritage is intimately anchored to place, terrain, language, culture, imagination, and lived spirituality. It does not proceed from hypothesis or theory; it is born of *praxis* and leaves mountains of evidence born of craft, set free in song. In this context, there is a Hebridean proverb that reflects timeless Wisdom: *"A short giving with gold,"* the islanders would say, *"but a long giving with song."*

Here we encounter the discerning nature of a traditional culture, one that *chooses beauty* over the many kinds of waste, distraction, or abstraction that are routinely operative for us today. In the year 2021, many of us are so embedded in late stages of consumerism that we do not know how to extricate ourselves from its maw. Few know the crofting skills needed to keep a roof overhead, and all are reliant upon others for procurement of the most basic goods and services. We turn to the *simulacrum* of the internet for purchase and are frequently stripped of personal relationship with the artisans and makers. Even theologians derive professional permission slips from external sources, for they are indebted to their degrees and universities for authorities conferred, unlike the conditions Evagrius describes. Later, they are ordained.

There were other ways of knowing a short time ago. Traditional cultures gave birth to the voice of authority through an arduous process of *mastery of craft*, and craft mastery knows no discrimination about gender. It knows, affirms, and confirms beauty and quality as they are linked together. The island crafts of shearing, carding, spinning, waulking, weaving, dyeing, thatching, tanning, smooring, churning, turfing (and more) were rhythmic in and of themselves and were further potentized by being embedded into the rhythm of daily life as lived in every croft. A characteristic element of artisanal labor entailed the capacities of meditative concentration and perseverance. Men, women, and youth often worked such handcrafts in patient solitude but also in small teams. As a result, the handcrafter's art taught one to focus, refine, and distill not only the substances in hand but also *truth*.

Proverb is truth distilled into a few soul-imbued words of wisdom. Whether working inside or outside, at loom or hearth, forge or field, shoreline or hedge, on land or sea, in solitude or in community, the rhythm of manual labor changed heart-beat and breath and contributed something major to the spirit-infused embodiment process of the traditional artisan. Whether one was working in fiber or hide, dulse or stone, meter or melody, any one could stop and apprehend what one knew in blood and bone: *The short giving in gold; the long giving in song.*

While wholly engaged in generative and meaning-filled labor, the wisdom uttered, embodied and sung is recognized as something summative, authoritative, alchemical, and providential. This harvesting concerned everything and everyone, and their Wisdom was spiritual content cooked down to essence, passed down from mouth to receptive heart more so than pen to page. How different from the development of doctrine or dogma, where the theological work occurs in the realm of thinking, commonly at a quiet desk in a tiny cell or an enclosed library carrel, removed

from the fresh air and open sky until taken to the powers that be. There is more, too.

At eventide, in the flickering light, the beauty of islander speech was amplified in the *ceilidh*, that hearthside social visit of music and storytelling that kept the moral imagination alive. Islander wisdom was generated in its own time outside of time, freely emerging from the creative womb when ripe or mature. It knew no institutional credentialling process or permission slip but relied instead on the self-authorizing fruitfulness of the effort. Each expression disclosed its innate intelligence, eloquence and value.

The cleanliness of this way of being speaks for itself and reflects the potential of peaceful collaborative co-existence. The wisdom of weaving together Creature, Spirit, and Nature has much to teach us.

Though I had not set out to do anything more than return to the music and ideas which I have loved for forty years, I returned to them because I remembered that they were profoundly Marian and profoundly Sophianic. In returning to them for this recital, I wound up observing and exploring something I can only describe *now* as a wonderfully transgressive operation. I did not have such conscious insight at the age of twenty-eight and twenty-nine, when I first purchased the MacLeod, the Shaw, the Fergusson, or the Carmichael, though the feeling-toned leap of the heart allowed me to know with certitude that I was holding books of great and radiant treasures. I employ the word transgressive today because it is so easy to see the ways and means that allowed life and people to jump over boundaries that existed for others who lived in heavily populated mainland Christian communities where the institution of the Church and the running of the State were enmeshed. In leaping over boundaries, *because they had to*, the Hebridean islander created and sustained that which was vital, life-giving, beauty-filled, and authentic.

It is easy to recognize an authority naturally and practically conferred in male and female working together harmoniously, mastering the various artforms mentioned. Their transgressive inclinations uncover a lived theology that was Marian, Sophianic, and inclusive. Not perfect by any means, but they had something we have surely lost. In addition to their artisanal handcrafts, the islanders had a preternatural acceptance of and sensibility toward all things Marian. Our Catholic stories of holiness depict how Mary exudes a fragrance, the scent of roses. She makes her presence known in the trailing of a scent which manifests from unknown or invisible sources. *She leaves her signature.* That is one of her keys. I can't help but think of Sister Joan's graceful and conscious acceptance of the assignment to be an irritating thorn. Her mantle hints of her relationship to Mary, the Mother, and the entire feminine *milieu.* Can you hear Benjamin Britten's *Ceremony of Carols*? The choir supported by that exquisite harp?

There is no rose of such virtue as is the rose that bare Jesu. *Alleluia!*

For in that rose contained was heaven and earth in little space. *Res miranda!*

I would love to bring this Hebridean culture ever closer to home for those who will never have the opportunity to work or live as an islander or crofter on a small plot of land. I can do this by virtue of the process of *weaving.*

Loom and shuttle provide entrée to a traditional artform with which I have been intimate for longer than I can remember, but a year ago, a very dear friend gifted me with a tapestry loom made of her own two hands. What a reminder! What a nudge! The Scottish are famous for their fiber arts, and I am not Scottish and have no Scottish ancestry, but dearly love their songs, prayers, proverbs, and wisdom. In loving, I have attempted to weave a *tapestry of recollection* echoing something of the ways in which their legacy has aided me in living with or making sense about the institutional rips and disconnects mentioned in the beginning of this recital.

Whether weaving tapestry or tweed, the warp and weft of cloth is neither haphazard nor arbitrary. Each vertical or horizontal choice is intentional yet leaves the artisan uniquely creative. The art of tapestry does not constellate a series of free associations, but, rather, is a way of weaving in which a full spectrum of expressions can be integrated into the progressively growing image.

"*Mediocrity suffers no greatness, shows beauty no mercy.*"
~ Henri de Lubac[28]

Anything natural from the environment may be used: fiber, straw, wool,

---

[28] Henri de Lubac, *Paradoxes of Faith.*

flax, cotton, silk, rush, tuft, moss, lichen, twig, shell, feather. So, too, have I incorporated a similar variety of expressions gathered from life as a praying, thinking, feeling Catholic, from being a Eucharistic person, connected to years of making and composing music, reading and studying in the spirit of contemplative scholarship, and attending the dying in their sick beds. Perhaps another kind of knee-woman. This tapestry recalls carefully gathered lines, phrases, salutations, and images drawn from hymn, poem, vision, prayer, song, croon, letter, and diary entries. These are the threads that provided a renewal of feminine strength and insight, while moistening the inner life. The lines you read here are woven as a result of holding and cherishing content for decades. An organically metamorphosing linguistic picture arises that is more recital than sequential or chronological scaffolding. These Hebridean ways were anything but perfect, they surely had as many peculiarities as any expression of Christianity, but I am unable to deny their purity, beauty, or inspiration.

Like so many feminine gifts, and like Our Lady herself, during the process of tapestry weaving, the vertical strands of any warp often begin to disappear, eventually becoming invisible as the shuttle's weft is layered into the whole. That is to say: the vertical lines of warp are foundational; they are backbone. As warp gradually becomes covered by the horizontal strands of the weft, we see that that which is strongest works *behind the scenes*. Not out front. Not at the top of the pyramid. There is no need to be a star. That security echoes the Balthasarian insight about the *disappearing nature* of someone who has truly been central to a mystery. A central source works assiduously for its own dissolution, not for its permanence.

The rhythms, colors, and textures more easily seen in the weft intimate something of human thirst and hunger. I hope the tapestry begins to awaken something of how urgently and widely we might revisit everything given: the wild hedgerow, the far field, shore and forest, blue dome of heaven, the proverb and the plaint. There are so many ways of knowing and they are freely available to all. These natural and diverse sources can be woven together now to make a new and living Ecclesial fabric that is strong, beautiful and provides needed protection and warmth. A truly whole Ecclesial fabric prepares us for the present and future, and finally, unfailingly provides us with untold riches with which to sustain life in body, soul and spirit.

Postlude

Birthing and dying (and everything in between) had unique prayers and ceremonies attached to them. The most remote islands might go years without a visit from a member of the clergy; and, for this reason, after a child is born he or she is immediately baptized by a special nurse, a mid-wife, and she is locally referred to as *the knee-woman*. This ceremony preserved an antiphonal way of singing-praying, in the home; that is to say, weaving sung blessing and thanksgiving back and forth across the room, where mother and child lay, in the air surrounding the child. The prayer was consistently Trinitarian: Father, Son, and Holy Spirit. The knee-woman blessing was called the *birth baptism* and was different from what might occur either eight days later or years later when a priest or priest-monk might visit. Other women present in the cottage where the pregnant woman was giving birth were called watching-women. They sang Amen after each phrase of the prayer sung by the knee-woman. On the larger islands where the clergy were easily present, the child was baptized by the priest eight days after the cottage birth had occurred and this second ritual was called the *clerical baptism*.

Rather than it being perceived as "more real" than the first, it was described as a sort of community deepening, manifesting a social dimension. Why? Because the family, friends, and neighbors all gathered together and participated in a way that can only happen in a culture where prayer and poetry converge as naturally as breathing. The infant was passed from person to person, clockwise, *"deiseil"* in a sunrise direction, and each person was required to express a unique wish for its welfare, preferably in rhymed verse instead of prose.

For the birth baptism, we have the following[29] recital from a woman from Barra:

> When the child comes into the world, the knee-woman puts three drops of water on the forehead of the poor little infant, who has come home to us from the bosom of the everlasting Father. The woman does the baptism in the name and in the reverence of the kind and powerful Trinity:
> The perfect Three of power, (*Amen!*) the little drop of the Father, (*Amen!*) the little drop of the Son, (*Amen!*) the little drop of the Spirit on thy little forehead, beloved one. (*Amen!*) To aid thee (*Amen!*) to guard thee (*Amen!*) to shield thee (*Amen!*) to surround thee (*Amen!*) to keep thee from the fays (*Amen!*) to sain thee from the gnome (*Amen!*) the little drop of the Three to shield thee from the sorrow, (*Amen!*) to fill thee with Their pleasantness (*Amen!*) to fill thee with Their virtue. (*Amen!*)

Later, when the mother was in solitude, (but as soon as possible after birth), she would go outside, ideally at noon, and face the sun, and touch the baby's brow to the earth. "It's the old Mothering,"[30] the locals said, the sacrament of Our Mother, in an ancient sense.

---

[29] In both Fiona Macleod and Carmichael.
[30] In both Fiona Macleod and Carmichael.

From Fiona Macleod, *The Divine Adventure*:

"The elderly, men and women of 80 and 90 years, sang a short hymn before praying, and did so in a unique islander way. They would step to an outbuilding, the lee of a knoll or the shelter of a dell so that they could not be seen or heard by anyone. Some walked as much as one or two miles to the seashore to join their voices with the pounding waves. They *intone in low tremulous unmeasured cadences, like the moving and moaning, the soughing and sighing of the ever murmuring sea on their shores.* They would sing this:

> I am bending my knee in the eye of the Father who created me, in the eye of the Son who purchased me, in the eye of the Spirit who cleansed me, in friendship and affection. To do on the world of the Three, as angels and saints do in heaven, each shade and light, each day and night, each time in kindness, give Thou us Thy Spirit.

There were prayers for lying down, for sleeping, for rising up, for bathing, to welcome Christ as the bringer[1] of evening stars: *Behold the Lightener of the stars on the crests of the clouds, and the choralists of the sky lauding Him!*

There were prayers to bless the bed, the loom, the cottage, the kindling, the seed, the quern, the boat, the flock.

There were prayers for sea-madness, sorrow, longing, and afflictions; for nursing mothers, for broken bones, marking of lambs, consecrating cloth, and consecrating the young men who went out to hunt.

Heisgeir was uninhabited by the time of the Shaw and Fergusson ethnographies, but it had been a culture of light and learning in by-gone days. One of the most thrilling discoveries I stumbled across was a hymn from Heisgeir that was a plaintive introspective melody and a meditation on the Beauty of Christ. If played by pipers, they would face the sun, and walk towards it, as it rose, with the light almost blinding them, but I also noticed that it could be profound on harp as well. This is the same island from which the many seal and silkie songs arise, where families understand themselves to be descendants of the silkies,[2] and for this reason do not ever hunt or kill the seals.

Every letter in the Gaelic alphabet is represented by a tree, and Beithe and Luis and Nuin are the Birch, the Rowan and the Ash.

Oran opened his eyes and declared there is no such great wonder as death, nor is Hell what it has been described. *Ifrinn* or *Ifurin*—either word is used—the *Gaelic Hell is the Land of Eternal Cold.*

Edward Calvert: I go inward to God; outward to the gods.[3]
Every morning, take your hat off to the beauty of the world.[4]
An old woman told me that when Christ was crucified, He came back to us[5] in Oisin of the Songs.

---

[1] Fiona Macleod and Carmichael
[2] Donald Fergusson, *From Farthest Hebrides.*
[3] Fiona Macleod
[4] Fiona Macleod
[5] Fiona Macleod

⊕
Recitals from Fiona Macleod

"... *our pillow is the arm of Mary...*"

"...*I dreamed that a harper came out of hill, at first so small that he seemed like a green stalk of a lily and had hands like daisies, and then so great that I saw his breath darkening the waves far out on the Hebrid sea. He played, till I saw the stars fall in a ceaseless, dazzling rain upon Iona ... and thousands upon thousands of white doves rise from the foam and fly down the four great highways of the wind....*"

"*Angel: ... You can have either beauty or music. .... Mother: Let the child have the melodious mouth and the harping hand....*"

"*Sometimes I dream of the old prophecy that Christ shall come again upon Iona,*[6] *and of that later and obscure prophecy which foretells, now as the Bride of Christ, now as the Daughter of God, now as the Divine Spirit embodied through mortal birth in a woman, as once through mortal birth in a Man, the coming of a new Presence and Power: and dream that this may be upon Iona, so that the little Gaelic island may become as the little Syrian Bethlehem. But more wise it is to dream, not of hallowed ground, but of the hallowed gardens of the soul wherein She shall appear white and radiant. Or, that upon the hills, where we are wandered, the Shepherdess shall call us home. From one man only, on Iona itself, I have heard an allusion to the prophecy as to the Savior who shall yet come: and he in part was obscure, and confused the advent of Mary into the spiritual world with the possible coming again to earth of Mary, as another Redeemer, or with a descending of the Divine Womanhood upon the human heart as a universal spirit descending upon waiting souls. .... My old nurse, Barabal, used to sing a strange "oran" to the effect that when St. Bride came again to Iona it would be to bind the hair and wash the feet of the Bride of Christ.*"

"*And a young Hebridean priest*[7] *told me once how "as our forefathers and elders believed and still believe, that Holy Spirit shall come again which once was mortally born among us as the Son of God, but, then, shall be the Daughter of God." The Divine Spirit shall come again as a Woman. Then for the first time the world will know peace. And when I asked him if it were not prophesied that the Woman is to be born on Iona, he said that if this prophecy had been made it was* doubtless symbolic, *but that this was a matter of no moment, for* She would rise suddenly in many hearts, and have her habitation among dreams and hopes."

"*This solitude is only apparent. It is a solitude filled with invisible presences. It is the painful condition of the deepest and purest communion.*"[8]

"*The other who spoke to me of this Woman who is to save was an old fisherman*[9]

---

[6] Fiona Macleod
[7] Fiona Macleod
[8] Henri de Lubac, *Paradoxes of Faith.*
[9] Fiona Macleod

of a remote island of the Hebrides, and one to whom I owe more than to any other spiritual influence in my childhood, for it was he who opened me to the Three Gates of Beauty.

Once this old man, Seumas Macleod, took me with him to a lonely haven in the rocks and held me as we sat watching the sun sink and the moon climb out of the eastern wave. I saw no one, but abruptly he rose and put me from him, and bowed his grey head as he knelt before one who suddenly was standing in that place. I asked eagerly who it was. He told me it was an Angel. The Angel was one soft flame of pure white, and below the soles of his feet were curling scarlet flames. He had come in answer to the old man's prayer. He had come to say that we could not see the Divine One whom we awaited. 'But you will yet see that Holy Beauty' said the Angel, and Seumas believed, and I too believed, and believe. He took my hand, and I knelt beside him, and he bade me repeat the words he said. And that was how I first prayed to Her who shall yet be the Balm of the World."

Diary entry when I was only twenty-five:

A young and earnest seminarian said to me: "*If the Church were truly Christian, it would be working assiduously toward its own dissolution, not building itself up for permanence.*" Am greatly shaken. This up-ends everything.

In loving memory of Bart van der Lugt, MD, knee-woman to those coming and going, to both the living and the dying.

The Chalice Well
March 17, 2021

A Solitary Place

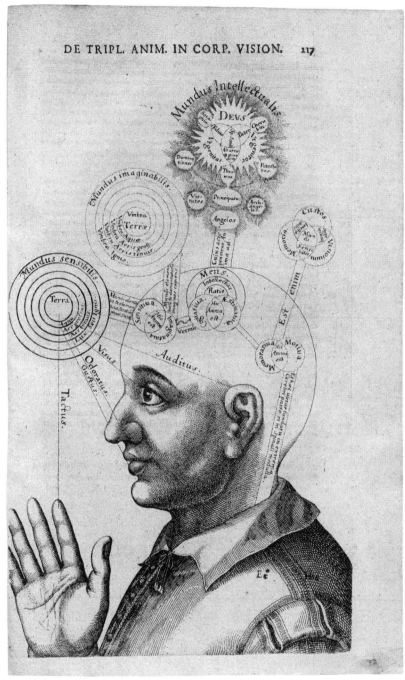

From Robert Fludd, *Utriusque cosmi historia*

ROBERT FLUDD

Thomas Whittier

the figure in profile has the kind eyes of a deer
lips full as roses barely break a smile
his brain is a diagram

Mundus sensibilis

Mundus imaginabilis

Mundus Intellectualis

these universes pour through
the fontanel's pulsing membrane   their

rays touch the transcendental brain divide into polarities of

imagination and sense   memory and death
knowing and guessing

where the spheres meet and reveal

the labia of the world

Robert Fludd has inscribed these words

hic
anima
est

here is the soul

God–In–Creation

The Sophianic Intuitions of Hildegard of Bingen

Miguel Escobar Torres

 N THE *De Divinis Nominibus* and the *De Mystica Theologia* of Pseudo-Dionysius stand out, in the first the cataphatic approach, the presence of God in creation, and the in second the apophatic approach, the only one possible if paradoxically we want to access what is by definition inaccessible, the absolutely transcendent God. Then, it is generally acknowledged that this double dimension in divinity is understandable from the categories of masculine and feminine: if the feminine dimension of God points to the immanence of God, the *God-in-creation*, the masculine dimension refers to transcendence, to the *God-beyond-creation*.

Consequently, a totalization of the feminine dimension and the oblivion of the masculine dimension inexorably leads to a confused pantheism. For its part, a unique attention to masculinity and a forgetting of femininity leads to the denial of the *God-in-creation*. In this sense, modernity, by giving excessive prominence to masculinity and neglecting and despising the feminine dimension, ends up blurring God and turning him into an alien spectator of human drama and whose possible intervention is conceived as a *supernatural* interference—normally illegitimate—as an *extraordinary* event, because the *quotidian* God is not there, he is not manifested: there is only the "natural." The rejection—and not the mere "forgetting"—of femininity opens a way for the appearance of a *Deus absconditus*, absent due to being apparently evicted. Modernity, therefore, is informed by the exile of God, and this exile of God is the necessary consequence of the denial of woman and femininity. All modern monstrosities—cities, universities, modern science, industrial capitalism, the State—originate from the rejection of the feminine.

In the attempt to find the origin of modern reason, in recent times the attention has fallen on the theory of the univocity of being of Duns Scotus. By identifying the germ of modernity in theology, modernity comes to be understood as a "parody of the liturgical order."[1] Secular reason is going to feed the illusion of a supposed autonomy of the created being with respect

[1] Catherine Pickstock, *After Writing: On the Liturgical Consummation of Philosophy* (Oxford, Blackwell Publishers, 2000), 121.

to the Creator, being the understanding of nature exhausted in nature itself, without contemplating a connection with divinity. Thus, by breaking the identity between God and being, Duns Scotus wrecks the platonic concept of participation and postulates an indeterminate, merely formal, and empty being in which both God and the created being participate. The most obvious consequences are that the created being stops participating in God and that God has become one more entity (exalted, yes, but an entity, after all). Another consequence, less evident but of great relevance, is that a paradoxical turn takes place that opens an unfathomable abyss between God and creation. In this way, God remains confined in a supernatural *topos* foreign to nature, while the world is stripped of the sacred, of the *quotidian* presence of the divine. Every theophany is seen as a violent irruption of a transcendent and arbitrary will. This desacralizing process renders the world opaque, superficial, meaningless; its main features are *transparency*, since there is no place for mystery in a world dominated by a "panoptic" rationality, and *availability*, since this lack of meaning invites this same reason, which contains the aggressiveness of the masculine character, to confer a merely functional and utilitarian sense.

There is no doubt that the Scotist theory of the univocity of being has a remarkable secularizing character. However, this non-transfigured and non-transfiguring gaze of reality was already manifested during the 11th century when the object of controversy was the Eucharist. Berengarius

of Tours was optimistic about the capacity of reason and dialectics as a means to discover the truth and did not hesitate to apply it to the mystery of the Eucharist. This submission of the Eucharist to this panoptic reason, on the one hand, denotes a lack of reverence for the mystery and, on the other, uses its efforts in a task manifestly doomed to failure. In any case, Berengarius's philosophical *attitude* was already as secularizing as the Scotist *theory* of the univocity of being. If there is something this attitude and this theory share, it is their inability to attend to the immanence of God, to the theophany that takes place in everyday life. Indeed, the excessive prominence of reason, masculine and possessing a certain amount of aggressiveness, led to ignorance of the femininity of God, and stimulated the extravagant theory that sees the world as the absence of God and, consequently, makes it transparent and available.

During the 12th century, this secularizing *attitude* remained in the intellectual life of the new burghs. Its main critic was Bernard of Clairvaux, who argued that trees and stones could be better teachers than books. Precisely in a more wooded environment, apart from the incipient modern cities, another type of thought arose not based on analytical or dialectical methods, an "unforeseen thought" that was not enthralled by the rediscovery of logical writings of Aristotle. Indeed, a typically feminine school of thought emerged, the *magistrae* tradition, whose main author is Hildegard of Bingen. This "unforeseen thought" will represent an alternative to the philosophy of the *magistri* from both an epistemic and metaphysical point of view.

From an epistemic point of view, the thought of the *magistrae* stands as an alternative to the dialectic of the cathedral schools, insofar as it operates with a different reason. The *magistri* dedicate their study *intra muros* to the liberal arts, those appropriate for the intellect, the properly human.

1. *The Seasons*

In contrast to this, the mechanical arts, also called vulgar or servile, tied man to the needs of the earth, to the world of sensible things, and that did not allow the fulfillment of man's intellectual *telos*. The cathedral schools emphasized the "liberating" character of these arts, since their abstract and universal character gave them independence from the toils of the earth. It is not misguided, therefore, to say that the *magistri* cultivated a *liberal reason*. While Duns Scotus's univocity of being introduced the secular from a metaphysical point of view, the liberal reason of the *magistri* already had a secularizing *attitude*. Liberal reason longs for liberation from natural ties, be it craft work or *undesirable* direct contact with the soil. The fact that this rationality developed in the cities is a sign of this desire for liberation. It is evident, on the other hand, that modern techno-science arises as a consequence of this rationality, since that desire for natural liberation has never been so satisfied as it is with cyberspace, the main superstition of our days. What better way to become independent from the world than to create a new world to consider it as the "kingdom of freedom"? (Illustration 1)

The thought of the *magistrae* is declared antidialectic, contrary to that of the cathedral schools. Its approach to reality is, therefore, radically different. Hildegard's opposition to liberal reason does not imply, however, an irrationalism, since the "liberal" is in no case consubstantial or a necessary feature of reason. The *magistrae* approach will be rational, too; but in this case, it is not a question of a *liberal* reason, but a *mystical* reason. The categorization of this reason as mystical does not pretend to bring this thought closer to the irrational excesses, lacking in all sobriety, which has taken place in modern times and is still present today, fueled by an unhealthy claim to individualism. The mystical of the reason of the *magistrae* suggests, instead, a capacity to recognize and revere the mystery as something present in the bosom of creation. Mystical reason, unlike liberal reason, had the gift of recognizing and contemplating cosmic cycles and their coincidence with liturgical cycles. This type of thinking views creation as an enormous cosmic liturgy. This would not be possible, however, if suspicion instead of wonder were at the origin of this approach. It is wonder which allows us to recognize the mystery in the very bosom of creation, and to revere it as *God-in-creation*.

In monasteries influenced by Hildegard, manual activities were an essential part of the life of both *magistrae* and female disciples. This artisan activity was also enriched with herbalism and agricultural activity, as well as a deep reading of Scripture. The proximity to the earth will be key to the development of the *magistrae's* thinking, especially Hildegard, since it will allow her to perceive the presence of God in the world as *viriditas*, and to conceive a creation impregnated with God and constantly nourished by him, as if being in his "mother's womb."

In short, wonder implies a contemplative openness towards the outside, a willingness to be absorbed by the wonders of creation, and an openness towards listening to the *vox de caelo*.

2. *Visio prima*

Hildegard herself confesses that it is Wisdom that instructs her. In these illuminations, Hildegard could read in simplicity, which differs from the methodical analysis typical of the cathedral schools, which had to dissect things—at least in a logical sphere—in order to understand them, to *appropriate them.* The Hildegardian approach to reality is what today we would call *wholistic*—catholic— because it apprehends the whole thing, alive, in simplicity. In contrast, analysis usually turns nature into a corpse, just as it tends to treat the living word as a dead letter, making admired contemplation of *viriditas* impossible. (Illustration 2)

A different epistemology results in a different metaphysics. Hildegard was able to appreciate the presence of God in the natural world, which turns her thought into a sophianic intuition. The third vision of the first part of *Scivias*, which contemplates the universe as if it were an egg, can shed light especially from the point of view of the divine feminine. Regarding the metaphor of the cosmic egg, certain authors have wanted to echo its clear allusion to the femininity of God, which is still true, but, in turn, run the risk of seeking the adulation of the dominant ideologies, blurring Hildegard's philosophy and turning her into the current prototype of a feminist woman. Nevertheless, the Hildegardian view of the universe cannot be understood without reference to *Caritas*, *Sapientia*, and *viriditas* ("greening power"). (Illustration 3)

The Hildegardian vision of the cosmic egg shows three aspects of the universe: unity, vitality, and nutrition.

The idea of the universe as an egg suggests that being is contained in a harmonic unity, in a coherent whole—although penetrated by "wild" forces—and that, therefore, it does not constitute a random agglomeration of juxtaposed objects, struck by senseless events. In the second vision of the first part of the *Liber divinorum operum* (LDO), Hildegard refers to the vision of the cosmic egg. In this new vision the universe is represented as a

3. *Wheel of the Universe*

4. *Cosmic Egg*

wheel contained in *Caritas* chest, the same dazzling figure whose vision she had previously developed. Here, Hildegard reflects on the idea of the world as a harmonic unity based on the interconnection of all things: "The wheel refers exactly to the action of turning, to the exact balance of the elements of the world."[1] Hildegard also refers to it in *O ignis Spiritus Paracliti*:

O current of power permeating all
In the heights upon the earth and
In all deeps:
You bind and gather
Everything together.[2] (Illustration 4)

The second aspect of the universe that its resemblance to an egg suggests is that it is *alive*, that this harmonic unity is also an *organic* unity. God,

[1] PL 97, 755D–756A.

[2] Saint Hildegard of Bingen, *Symphonia* (Ithaca: Cornell University Press, 1998), 148.

embracing creation, breathes life into it, makes it breathe and grow. This is how Barbara Newman puts it: "Nothing is more distinctively Hildegardian than this sense of universal life, of a world aflame with vitality."[3] The *vox de caelo* reveals to Hildegard in the first vision of the LDO that God has not created anything that is not alive:

> I, the highest and fiery power, have kindled every spark of life, and *emit nothing that is deadly*. I decide in all reality. With my lofty wings I fly above the globe: with wisdom I have rightly put the universe in order. I, the fiery life of divine essence, am aflame beyond the beauty of the meadows. I gleam in the waters. I burn in the sun, moon and the stars. With every breeze, as with invisible life that contains everything, I awaken everything to life.[4]

God has created nothing that is not alive, and his breath is an invisible life that contains everything and that renews life constantly. This consideration reinforces the idea of the universe as an enormous cosmic liturgy, in which all things emit songs of praise to their Creator, as the psalmist claims: "*Coeli enarrant gloriam Dei*" (Psalm 19). The universe, similar to an egg, is a cosmos that is alive and whose cosmic cycles represent its breathing in a sort of doxological chant. In other words, liturgy beats in the depths of creation.

To the extent that the world "breathes God," it also feeds on Him. Thus, God is the *nutrix* of the world. If there is something that the vision of the cosmic egg suggests about the immanence of God, it is his continuous nourishment that breathes and maintains life in all beings. Indeed, an egg contains an embryo, an incipient being that is called to develop and that, to do this, must be nourished, cultivated, fed. In the vision of the cosmic egg, God sustains and *nurtures* the world through the elements. There is already something divine, even sophianic, in the *heat*, because, when she speaks of the meaning of the bright fire and the skin of darkness, Hildegard points out that is God who "burns *everywhere*." Air appears in the form of "wind" and "whirlwinds," diffusing throughout the instrument the heat that is given off by the brilliant fire that surrounds and comprises the egg, as well as its radiant light. God not only sustains, but *is* in creation, He is as immanent as He is transcendent. And this *God-in-creation* is represented through the female figure of *Sapientia*, understood as *creatrix*, as Barbara Newman explains: "As creatrix, Hildegard's Sapientia is no unmoved mover, ordering the Universe from on high or even (…) molding the nascent world in almighty hands. On the contrary, she creates the cosmos by existing within it, her ubiquity expressed through the image of ceaseless or circular motion."[5] The same author later points out that *Sapientia* is rather "an ambience enfolding it [the world] and quickening it from within."[6] How different is the Hilde-

---

[3] Barbara Newman, *Sister of Wisdom: St. Hildegard's Theology of the Feminine* (Aldershot: Scholar Press, 1987), 67.
[4] PL 197, 743BC.

[5] Barbara Newman, *Sister of Wisdom*, 64.
[6] Ibíd., 65.

gardian conception of God from Descartes's *Deus ex machina*!

Likewise, water has its own sphere in a circle of "watery air and white skin," but it also spreads and spills over the entire instrument thanks to the diffusing action of the wind and whirlpools. The water, which Hildegard links to baptism, "spreads everywhere, thanks to divine inspiration, bringing to the universe the spring that brings health to believers."[7] We must highlight the ubiquity of the aqueous element and the universality of baptism—the entire globe!—which is given because of the unity that Hildegard appreciates between liturgy and cosmos. The cosmos is, therefore, liturgical, sacramental. Air does not only extends baptism to all creation, but it also makes the universe shake, communicating sin everywhere. There is no place in the universe that remains indifferent to the sacraments or unscathed by sin. Also in the vision of the wheel of the universe, Hildegard provides two circles of fire, a circle of pure ether and two circles of air, all the circles being interlaced, suggesting the organic unity of the sphere: "The highest circle of all diffused its light to the rest of the circles, while the circle of humid air soaked all the others with its humidity,"[8] being all "united among them, without any empty space."[9] Or, in other words, no room for the secular.

Finally, the center of the egg is occupied by the earth, a "sand globe," where "man, imbued with deep understanding, who lives in the midst of the forces of divine creation, made of clay of the earth with great glory and so united to the energies of creation that it cannot be separated from them, because the elements of the world, founded to serve man, render him vassalage."[10] The centrality of man in creation is in Hildegard very different from modern anthropocentrism, which sees man as the tyrant of the universe who must subdue and plunder everything. The primacy of the human being in creation is not based on the illusory confrontation between the I and the Not-I—to put it in Fichtean terms—where the I consists of a *separate* subject and *opposed* to nature, which must be overcome. Indeed, Hildegard does not contemplate either this opposition or the illusory hypostatization of man with respect to nature. The Cartesian postulation of a *res cogitans* that can be understood outside of space and time and even apart from the body itself, is completely strange to Hildegard. Man does not occupy the center of the universe because he opposes it, but because all cosmic forces converge in him. Things, it is true, render him vassal, but man is rooted in the earth—he is made of clay with great glory—he is united with the energies of creation, and, therefore, cannot be separated from them. Hildegard's anthropological conception is integral, *wholistic*, and therefore truly *catholic*. (Illustration 5)

Likewise, *Caritas*, like *Sapientia*, alludes to the femininity of divine immanence, and can be understood as *anima mundi*, as "consort of God" or as an archetype of the Virgin Mary.

[7] CC, XLIII, 14, 268-269.
[8] PL 197, 751D.
[9] Ibíd., 751C.
[10] Ibíd., 16, 190–300.

5. Caritas

Sapientia, for her part, also represented from a female figure—which distinguishes her in a certain sense from the Second Hypostasis of the Trinity—can be conceived as "consort of God," but also as *creatrix* and as an image of the Virgin Mary. The *quasi* identification of these two figures is manifest, although *Caritas* is closer to the hypostasis of the Holy Spirit and *Sapientia* to the hypostasis of the Son, without, of course, either of the two being identified with them, since the hypostases of the Holy Spirit and the Son are part, together with the Father, of the transcendent Trinity, while *Caritas* and *Sapientia* must be understood within the framework of God's immanence. These two sophianic figures are best described in the songs of the *Symphonia*. Hildegard specifically dedicates a song of praise to the divine *Sapientia*, which permeates all Creation:

> O power of Wisdom!
> You encompassed the cosmos,
> Encircling and embracing all
> In one living orbit
> With your three wings:
> One soars on high,
> One distills the earth's essence,
> And the third hovers everywhere.
> Praise to you, Wisdom, fitting
> praise![11]

The first vision of the LDO, which represents the female figure that will contain the wheel of the universe in her chest in the next vision, is even more eloquent than the allegory of the cosmic egg. If the consideration of the egg-shaped universe suggested a

maternal or feminine aspect of God, the wheel of the universe will go one step further, presenting the universe contained in the breast of a female figure identified with *Caritas*, the love of God. *Caritas* embraces, contains, enlivens, and nourishes all Creation.

Meanwhile, *Sapientia* maintains some correspondence with the Church, "Christ's wife," of which Hildegard also speaks in terms of motherhood. It is not strange, therefore, that the Church is an image of the Virgin Mary—as the hymn "O Ecclesia" shows—just as this is the personification of *Sapientia* that gives birth to the Word, whom she feeds and cultivates in her bosom. *Caritas*, also an archetype of Mary, is described in maternal terms as well.

Consequently, the Virgin Mary occupies a central position in Creation, as the personification of *Caritas* and *Sapientia*. In addition, allusions to *viriditas* abound in Hildegard's descriptions of Virgin Mary, which is called *viridissima virga* (the greenest branch*)*, *virga mediatrix* (mediating branch), *virga ac diadema* (crowned branch), *frondens virga* (leafy branch), *suavissima virga* (the softest branch) and *splendidissima gemma* (the most splendid gem). The first thing that stands out is the characterization of Mary based on elements of natural exuberance, branches, gems, trees, etc., which not only makes the Virgin related to the earth, but also makes the earth sacred itself. On the other hand, the allusion to Mary as *mediatrix* delves into the metaphysical correspondence of the Virgin with Sophia, while suggesting that she occupies the place of the middle (*metaxu*), the bridge between the nat-

[11] My translation. Saint Hildegard of Bingen, *Symphonia…*, 100.

ural and the supernatural, between the created and the uncreated. In this sense, already in the context in which Hildegard was inserted, the idea of a pre-existence of Mary with respect to creation was very present. The concept of *viriditas* is, therefore, linked to *Sapientia*, *Caritas* and the Virgin Mary; all these seem to be situated in that mediating place, the "suspended middle." As usual, the poetic expressiveness of the Hildegardian songs reflect more appropriately the meaning of *viriditas*, as in the case of the song *O nobilisssima viriditas*:

> O most noble greenness,
> you are rooted in the sun,
> and you shine in bright serenity
> in a sphere
> no earthly eminence
> attains.
> You are enfolded
> in the embraces of divine
> ministries.
> You blush like the dawn
> and burn like a flame of the sun.[12]
> (Illustration 6)

increata—prior to Creation—but also a *Sophia creata*. The movement of the *Sophia increata* is descending (agapeic); that of the *Sophia creata*, ascending (erotic). The divine Sophia contains, embraces, and nurtures creation; creatural Sophia contains, embraces, and nurtures God. Therefore, God is called to be everything in everyone: that is, to be born and grow in us, God must be cultivated, contained, embraced, fed. Then, the *Sophia creata* is also a *nutrix*, although it is not about God feeding Creation, but about Creation cultivating divinity. The *Sophia increata* has an evident primacy over the *creata*; however, it is no less true that the created being is also called to be a co-creator. To put it simply, God nurtures Creation so that Creation nurtures God. In this sense, Angela of Foligno, a Franciscan mystic who withdraws from secularizing Franciscan *magistri*, constitutes the perfect complement to Hildegard when she claimed that "the world is pregnant with God!"

6. *Sapientia*

Nevertheless, as Boehme suggests, there is not only a divine Sophia, but also a creaturely one. There is a *Sophia*

If Hildegard conceived the world as being in God, Angela's vision proposes a God who is *in* the world. And the word "in" implies, on the one hand, presence, a *being-there*, and not

---

[12] Hildegard of Bingen, *Symphonia…*, 218–19.

just a mere symbol that speaks of traces and strips the things themselves of light; and, on the other hand, it alludes to the present time, since the relationship of the universe with God is not a mere relationship of origin, of a remote origin. The world is not only *from* God but is *in* God. And, vice versa, God—without ceasing to be transcendent—is *in* the world, he spills over creation, and his presence nourishes it, and nature, exuberant, shines with the noblest *viriditas*. But God, in turn, grows within creation; the created being nurtures God, culti-vates him, makes him grow and manifest. The visions of Hildegard of Bingen and Angela of Foligno intuit Sophia, the *God-in-creation*, her feminine face, in the double divine and creative dimension. The cosmos is a temple, receptacle of the divine, which harbors Sophia within itself and which sings the praises of the Creator. And the Virgin Mary, *theotokos*, condenses the entire universe in her person; she is the image of the cosmic liturgy, because, as Mary was in her time, also the world is pregnant with God.

THE SECRET OF THE NIGHT
(for Novalis)

Bill Trusiewicz

When the twilight sky out-breathes
the last trace of daylight
into the heaven's deep whorl,

And a jewel be-speckèd brilliance
alone articulates
the dark celestial dome,

Is it not then, out of night's holy
womb—that true vision is born?

Disclosing the secrets hidden
Behind the veil of the day's deceit?

What flaming joys, what holy desires
are so expressed in those fires
that burn—yet are not consumed!

The sum of Earthly memory
spans but a few ticks
of this Immortal Clock.

No, death has no power here
where burns the eternal flame

Pure as gold
and without smoke.

Burning Bush, Tyler DeLong, woodcut

Honor Your Father & Your Mother

The Law of Continuity or The Life of Tradition

Valentin Tomberg
Translated by James Wetmore

> *Honor your father and our mother, so that you may*
> *live long in the land the* LORD *your God is giving you.*
>
> Exodus 20:12

I

Divine Foundation & Archetype of Fatherhood & Motherhood

 HE MOST PRECIOUS AND necessary experience we may have on earth from our earliest childhood is that of love, specifically of parental love, without which we would not even be able to make a start in life and remain living. As is well known, the newborn child will not thrive unless loving, caring, protecting hands receive and cherish it. Nourishment, warmth, and protection, already given in the mother's body before birth, continue to be needed by the child in various ways after birth also. Moreover, the child needs to be heard, and to hear the voices of others. For the child's development, language is necessary, for it requires contact, communication, interaction, which are fundamental for the first stirrings of thinking, understanding, and being understood.

In the further course of this continuing concern for the unfolding of the child's body and soul, the distinction between mother-love and father-love begins to emerge more and more clearly. The tendency of mother-love is to maintain an enveloping quality that "carries" the child further, so to speak, until the full-term of maturity is attained. The tendency of father-love is to stimulate and accelerate the child's development and independence. Father-love sees in the child an "heir" to continue his life's work, to fight for the same ideal and further the same task. Mother-love remains true to the image of the original mother–child bond during the pre-natal period, that of enveloping, protecting, and sustaining the child. Mother-love seeks to protect the child from life's roughness, to preserve it from every disappointment and every sorrow, to turn it's every tear into a smile. The love of the mother holds the child in her embrace, pressed to her heart, for decades on end—perhaps until death and beyond. Embracing the child is not foreign to father-love, but it shows itself less often: perhaps in solemn moments of heartfelt sharing, of grateful mutual acknowledgement, of taking pride in one another.

Parental love, the love bestowed by *both* father and mother, represents the most precious, the most meaningful experience a child can have on earth. Parental love is the dowry the child will carry throughout life; it is the "capital" of soul warmth and light upon which the developing individual can draw his whole life long. Parental love quite naturally prepares us by way of analogy to comprehend divine love, or at least to gain some presentiment of it, so that we may hope to understand the depth and truth of St. John's words: "God is love, and he who abides in love abides in God, and God abides in him" (1 Jn. 4:16). For, as God is love, so must the foundation and archetype of all love, including parental love, be in God.

Now, if all fatherhood has its origin and foundation in the Godhead, if therefore father-love corresponds in essence to the love of God the Father (as all Christians believe, even the Protestants, who have separated themselves from the stream of living tradition of the Church), how can we justify leaving unanswered the question whether motherhood and, correspondingly, mother-love, have their origin and foundation in the Godhead also? Are we to deny that mother-love is rooted in the divine, has its archetype in the divine, and esteem only

father-love as worthy of a divine archetype?

A categorical answer to this question is to be found in the prayer life and devotions of the tradition of the Church. Indeed, acknowledgment of the maternal principle plays a fundamental role in the religious practices of both Catholic and Orthodox Christianity. The praying the rosary has for centuries been intrinsic to the religious life of the Catholic Church. And essential to the rosary is the fact that its sequence of prayers appeal *alternately* to *father-love* (in the form of the "Our Father" with which each set of rosary prayers dedicated to the various "mysteries" begins) and to *mother-love* (in the form of the ten "Hail Marys" that follow). In the Orthodox Church, veneration of the Mother of God goes so far that in the liturgy the hymn is sung:

> "Truly it is worthy to bless Thee,
>   the Theotokos,[1]
> ever blessed and pure, and the
>   Mother of our God.
> Thee, who art more honorable
>   than the Cherubim,
> and incomparably more glorious
>   than the Seraphim;
> who incorruptibly didst bear God,
>   the Word,
> verily the Theotokos we magnify."

This means that the Mother of God ranks above the highest of the angelic hierarchies, the Cherubim and Seraphim, and so belongs to the suprahierarchical realm of the Godhead. Now, above these highest of the hier-

---

[1] *Theotokos*, Greek for "God-bearer," understood as Mother of God, that is, the Virgin Mary.

archies, the Cherubim and Seraphim, stands the eternal Trinity of God. Before saying more on this theme, however, it must be emphasized that what we are speaking of now is not a matter of Church *dogma*. Rather, we are pointing out the degree of *devotion* displayed by Orthodox believers toward Mary as "Holy Mother": for the hearts of the faithful in Russia (the land where the author of these pages was born and raised) Mary is the Queen of Hearts because she is the symbol and archetype of maternal love. The Orthodox Church also calls Mary "Queen of Heaven" and "Queen of the Angels."

Turning now to the Latin liturgy, we find that in the readings for Mary's birth, these words of the eternal Wisdom are given her to speak:

> The LORD created me at the beginning of his work. . . . When he established the heavens, I was there, when he drew a circle on the face of the deep . . . rejoicing in his inhabited world and delighting in the human race. (Proverbs 8:22, 27, 31)

Medieval depictions have Mary taking her seat next to the exalted Christ and receiving the crown. The piety of the people associates the veneration of the Heart of Mary with the veneration of the Heart of Jesus. Instead of taking offence at this, should we not follow the honored rubric *lex orandi, lex credend*,[2] and ask instead what truth may stand behind this insight that the maternal nature looking upon us in the person of Mary is in truth primordially rooted in the depth of the Godhead?

The Jewish kabbalistic tradition also answers the question whether by nature and primordial foundation mother-love is divine with a resounding yes. The Kabbalah teaches in accordance with the verse "God created man in His image and likeness . . . male and female He created them" that God has two aspects, the masculine and the feminine. It characterizes these two aspects as "countenances": the "greater" and the "lesser" countenance. The greater countenance or "ancient of days" is present in the sephirah *kether* (the crown) as the reflection of the androgynous Godhead, named *ain soph* (the unlimited). From *kether* a process of polarization gives rise to masculine and feminine principles. The right branch of the polarization is the masculine principle, and the left branch is the feminine principle.

Thus, through its reflected presence in *kether* in the world of emanation (*olam ha atziluth*), and its subsequent polarization in that world into the sephirot *chokmah* (wisdom) and *binah* (understanding), *ain soph* (the unlimited) comes to manifestation as both father and mother of creation.

Following this polarization further in the world of creation (*olam ha briah*), which is centered upon the sephirah *tiphareth* (beauty), we find the masculine principle characterized as king (*melekh*) or holy king, and the feminine principle—*shekinah* (glory), or the divine presence in created being—characterized as *matrona* or

---

2 *Lex orandi, lex credenda* ("the law of what is prayed is the law of what is believed") is a motto in Christian tradition which means that prayer and belief are integral to each other and that liturgy is not distinct from theology.

queen. Just as the king (*melekh*) is likened to the sun, so is the *matrona* likened to the moon as the reflection of ideal beauty. *Matrona* is also called Eve, for as the text relates, Eve is the Mother of all things, and everything that exists on earth suckles at her breast and is blessed by her.[3]

The "king" and the "queen" we are speaking of, who are also called the "two countenances," constitute a pair whose task is to bestow upon the world ever renewed graces, and through their union to continue the work of the creation—in other words, to sustain it everlastingly.

According to the *Zohar* the soul, viewed in its purest essence, is rooted in understanding (*binah*), which is the highest "mother" principle. If the soul is to be masculine in quality, it moves on from *binah*, passing through the principle of grace or expansion (*chesed* or *gedulah*). If the soul is to be feminine in quality it moves on from *binah*, taking into itself the principle of justice or contraction (*geburah*). Finally, through the union of the "king" and the "queen" (which union, as the text relates, is, for the generation of the soul, what the male and female are for the procreation of the body), the soul then enters the world in which we as mankind live (*malkuth*).[4]

In light of kabbalistic teaching, found also in Hasidism (upon which Martin Buber is an authority), we may summarize as follows the metaphysical-religious foundation for the commandment "Honor your father and your mother":

Creation (that is, the world), owes its existence to the love of the eternal Father and the love of the eternal Mother. Out of their union proceeds "as Light from Light, God from God" the Son and the Daughter, designated as the holy "king" and "queen," who together direct the work of Creation, guiding it to ever deeper levels of interiorization. However, the dimension of interiorization does not stand under the aegis of *becoming*—of coming into existence and thereafter sustaining what has come into existence. Rather, the dimension of interiorization aligns with the *blessing* that proceeds from the interiorizing (hallowing) Holy Spirit, who proceeds in turn from the Father and the Son. Corresponding, however, to the blessing of the *transcendent*, interiorizing divine Holy Spirit of the Holy Trinity, there is as well the *immanent* Presence of interiorizing blessing—which we may call the "Holy Soul," "the Virgin of Israel," or the "Soul of the community of Israel." She is the deeply moving and touching figure (portrayed by Martin Buber) of the Weeping Virgin who accompanies the chosen people into exile ("exile" not merely in a geographical sense). It is She who stands behind the wailing wall in Jerusalem, behind the lamentation of mankind.

In this respect, kabbalistic tradition *extends* the teaching of the Holy Trinity, acknowledging that father-love and mother-love are of the same divine origin and value, as presupposed by the commandment: "Honor your father and your mother."

In light of this extended teaching, the Three-in-One of the Trinity,

[3] *Zohar, Idra Zuta, ad finem* [that is, toward the end of the "Small Assembly," a text included in the Zohar], Ed.

[4] *Zohar*, III, 7.

becomes the Six-in-One of "Double" Trinity. But even so, the fundamental conception of monotheism is in no way lost but remains just as valid in light of this Double Trinity as it has always remained in the Christian doctrine of the Trinity, with its Three in the Unity of One God.

To the triangle of Father, Son, and Holy Spirit, then, we here add the triangle of Mother, Daughter, and Holy Soul: two triangles belonging inseparably together. Joined thus they represent the six-pointed Star of David, or (according to kabbalistic tradition), the Seal of Solomon.

Regrettably, the National Socialists chose this symbol to brand the Jews as a lesser race. Our great hope is that the above considerations will open up a pathway of thinking and sympathetic understanding along which this symbol will come to be honored again in its true depth and holiness. For it is a symbol of *faithfulness* to the commandment: "Honor your father and your mother—as in heaven so also upon the earth."

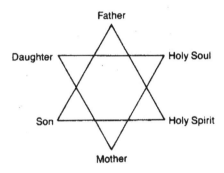

II

The Law of Living Tradition

"That your days may be long in the land which the Lord, your God, gives you"

Our native human reason would be unable to make anything of the world as empirically given if it did not have at its disposal the three fundamental categories, or ways of looking at and ordering experience that we call "space," "time," and "causality." The most concrete and simplest description of these three categories would be: for space, that things are next to each other; for time, that things succeed each other; and for causality, that things exist on account of each other.[5] Lacking these three categories, our reason would lack orientation; indeed, it would be unable even to frame questions, for all inquiry pre-

---

[5] These three categories are expressed in the German in the lapidary expressions: *das Nebeneinander, das Nacheinander, das Wegeneinander.* ED

supposes a *where* (whither, whence), a *when* (before, after), and a *why* (how, to what purpose). Furthermore, these three categories hold true not only for the empirical outer world but for the realm of metaphysics, morality, values, and faith also.

For example, the disciples' question to Jesus regarding the man born blind, whether his blindness was owing to his own or to his parents' sin, presupposed the law of moral causality. In fact, it did so on two possible counts: either in the sense of the Mosaic commandment of the "sins of the fathers afflicting the children," or in the sense of the guilt of the man born blind himself. The latter possibility corresponds to the conception of moral causality generally held by the peoples of the East, called *karma*, according to which individuals bear the consequences of their own deeds, whether noble or ignoble, not their children or children's children. The deeper sense of the disciples' question, then, was whether the fate of the man born blind stemmed from his parents' guilt or from karma, that is from his own guilt in a prior existence before birth? And the answer they received was notable in establishing that the destiny of the man born blind was neither the consequence of guilt on the part of his ancestors (in the sense of retribution through heredity) nor atonement for his own guilt from a time preceding his birth. The destiny of the man born blind was to be explained neither by moral causality working through the generations nor by individual karma. It occurred, rather, in order that "God's works might be made manifest in him" (John 9:3). This means that the cause

of his blindness lay not in the *past* but in the *future*. It was not a matter of past heredity or karma but of *providence*. But even so, both the disciples' question and the Master's reply *do* still pertain to the category of causality, for the decrees of providence are likewise causal in nature and have their effects as well, but with the *distinguo* that in the case of providence the causes and effects come from the future, not from the past. The deep truth of the Master's answer is that the cause of the man born blind's malady did not originate from human subjects (whether his parents' "guilt" or his own), but from a suprahuman Subject—*God's* providence.

But it is not only the category of *causality* that can be understood in a purely moral sense. The same holds true of the categories of *time* and *space*. When for example we pray the opening salutation of the Lord's Prayer: "Our Father, who art in *heaven*," we do not mean by heaven the *external* space of planets and stars, but *moral* space, that is, a space in which nobility corresponds to "height" and baseness to "depth." Similarly, the second part of the commandment: "Honor your father and your mother, that your *days may be long* in the land which the Lord your God gives you," is not meant to hold out the prospect of living for a long *time* at a particular spatially-determined place (such as a vineyard or other place of work), but the *enduring* of what is for you most important in life—your ideas, ideals, and goals—within the sphere of influence granted them by God. In other words, in the text referred to it is not a question of promising a protracted earthly life in some locale, but of assuring the uninterrupted impact and influence of contents and values, within their destined domain, of matters associated with earthly life. What this commandment actually speaks to, then, is the law of longevity of *tradition* in the domain peculiar to it.

Tradition is the moral content of *time* in the same way that fair retribution is the moral content of *causality*. Things following upon one another conceived merely as succession (that is, purely as time) remain inessential and morally hollow if not joined by the marrow of tradition. Tradition is the "moral spine" of time. It is the ever-present joint between what came before and what follows after, whether in terms of progress and regression, or of ascent and decline. Culture and civilization are simply other ways of saying tradition.

Science, however, assigns to time the very different meaning of *development* in the sense of biological *evolution*, which rests upon two factors: conservation through the law of heredity and so-called mutations changing the course of heredity (novel factors that from time to time impinge upon otherwise conservative hereditary transmission). Speaking more generally, the theory of biological evolution presupposes three things: the above-mentioned principle of conservation through heredity (lacking which the existence of the species would be inconceivable); the above-mentioned occurrence of mutations (lacking which there would be no progress, and so, in fact, no *evolution*); and *time* itself, understood here as the only and all-powerful "master teacher" that in the course of

empirical experience and random occurrence affords incalculable latitude for natural selection, adaptation, and breeding. Time in this sense *is* evolution. Belief in evolution, then, is tantamount to belief in time. But in the present case of biological theory, belief in evolution ("belief in time") implies, not higher moral development, but *survival of the fittest.* According to this teaching, what evolution aspires to through its school of trial and error is the capacity to adapt to, or to dominate, the environment. From this point of view, then, the evolution of mankind brings forth, not saints and sages, but mechanics and engineers; for those equipped with such technical capacities are assuredly far better *fitted* to the struggle for existence.

Seen in this light, the official Soviet Union promotion of authors as "engineers of the psyche" is nothing but a strategy to deracinate the authorial role and transplant it into a general scheme of functional utility. The author's task becomes thereby, not serving truth, goodness, and beauty, but awakening psychological forces useful, indeed indispensable, for advancing plans not only to quantitatively stimulate production, but to simultaneously galvanize the qualitative commitment of the entire society to willingly implement such plans. Communists are adherents of evolution in just this sense and for this reason have no use for truth, goodness, and beauty as ends in themselves. For them, "truth" is what is useful, "good" is what is well-adapted, "beautiful" is what lends a pleasing facade to some utilitarian function. For them a new railroad being laid in Siberia should be no mere construction project, but treated as an article of faithful belief, to be celebrated in song, daubed on canvas, and movingly retold in literature as yet another jewel in the crown of the communist edifice. In sum, time, conceived as evolution, is amoral, and the consequences of amoral ideas are generally immoral.

One relates to the world in a very different way when time is conceived, not as evolution, but as the bearer of living tradition. For when conceived as past, present, and future, time is transmuted into a morally-connected, organic whole. Within this whole the *past* (the "fathers" and "mothers") is honored, valued, and cherished as the inexhaustible source of the living water of tradition, which flows into the *future*, while at the same time every *present* moment offers the possibility and opportunity both to reflect upon the *values* of tradition recalled from the past and to look to the future in hopeful anticipation of the ripening fruits of tradition.

Essential to living tradition is its resistance to the powers of forgetting, sleep, and death. For these three powers are all expressions of a *single* principle: that of *passing away in the course of time.*

Now, general life experience teaches that time as such effects a tendency toward forgetting, falling asleep, and death, and that every response to time, every reliance upon time, every compromise with time, opens wide the gate leading inevitably to forgetting, sleep, and death. In the biblical text of the conversation at Caesarea Philippi, the following passage is usually rendered: "and the gates of *hell* (Hades) will not prevail against it"

(Matt. 16:18). However, *Hades*, which corresponds to the Hebrew *She'ol*, does not mean the place or the condition of the damned, but simply the kingdom of the dead, or simply death. Gates of death, then, are in effect entrances and exits along the course of *time*, all of which lead to death. The pledge in Jesus Christ's words, "You are Peter and on this rock I will build my Church, and the gates of hell will not overcome it" contains the mandate, the promise, and the blessing of freedom from *time*—that is, the power to *resist* the tendencies of death. In other words, this mandate, promise, and blessing pledges that, for as long as the Church remains firmly set upon the See of Peter as a living tradition, it will remain immune to the death-dealing influences of time. Temporal influences will never overcome the Church, never gain the upper hand within the Church, for as long as the See of Peter fulfills Christ's pledge to maintain the living tradition, which is the Church, and, by doing so, to protect it from passing away.

Every living tradition is based upon two forces working together: the sustaining force of *memory*, oriented toward the past; and the force of *hope*, oriented toward the future. The former preserves the past from being forgotten; the latter gives shape to the future as the path toward fulfillment. In other words, the motherly principle preserves tradition and the fatherly principle guides it toward its future goal. The continuing viability or life span of tradition, of every tradition, is bound up with the commandment "Honor your father and your mother."

The faculty of memory upon which the life of tradition depends is not mere recollection, the practise of recalling ideas from the past. Rather, it is the ability of the soul in all its fullness, to bring the past alive in the present, to *make it present*.

So, for example, the devotional practice of the fourteen stations of Christ's Way of the Cross, which according to tradition the most holy Virgin Mother herself introduced, is no mere memory exercise, an effort to commit to memory what happened at that time and in what order, but a striving to *experience*, as in the present, what is unforgettable about the Way of the Cross.

Also, Christ's last words at the institution of the holy sacrament at the Last Supper, "Do this in memory of me," indicate that all the sacraments are likewise revivifications in the present of what took place in the past. In the holy sacrament at the altar, remembrance becomes the divine-magical act of transubstantiation, an act relating to the *real*, not the merely *recalled*, presence of the body and blood of the Redeemer. What once took place, takes place now, in the present. In the sacrament, memory does not set out on a journey into the past, but instead summons the past into the present, evoking something from the realm of forgetting, sleep, and death. Such memory as this comes to bear the very power that sounded forth in the call of the Master, "Lazarus, come forth!" And let us not forget that this latter call proved equal to its task. Memory becomes divine magic. It becomes a miracle of great love and faith. In this sense, the words: "Do this in memory of me"

truly mean: "Do this, so that I may be *present*." For, need we add? the Son of Man is Lord also over time.

However, tradition could not remain viable for long merely on the strength of the sustaining and revivifying power of remembrance of the *past*: for this it requires *will* aimed at perfecting the tradition, at shaping the *future*. Such will revealed itself concretely in such figures as St. Augustine and St. Ignatius of Loyola; perhaps in all founders of orders. St. Augustine, with utmost loyalty and devotion, held fast to what Mother Church treasured in memory. He held fast also to her authority, which he considered highest and most decisive. But even so, he also depicted the great *future* goal of the Church and of the spiritual history of mankind in his work *De Civitate Dei* (*The City of God*), a work that laid a foundation for the history of philosophy as well. As for St. Ignatius, he established an order and a method of instruction aimed at educating others toward becoming worthy contenders in the quest to bring Augustine's "City of God" to realization. As is well known, the Rules of the Augustinian Order were adopted as the basis for the life and activity of the "Society of Jesus" founded many centuries later by St. Ignatius.

What, in truth, do the Rules of a spiritual order amount to? They express the *will* of its founder, the "father" of the order (to whom his "sons" freely pledge obedience), which is oriented toward a goal, toward an ideal. By fulfilling the will of their "father," that is, by taking the Rules as the content of their own will, they "honor their father." This, then, is the other side of the secret of the longevity of tradition as expressed more fully in the commandment: "Honor your father and your mother, that your days may be long in the land that the Lord your God gives you."

It is a fact that the religious orders of the Catholic Church (the Orthodox Church does not have orders properly speaking but individual monastic communities that to a greater or lesser extent continue the tradition of the Cenobite communities of the desert fathers) reveal an astonishing life span surpassed only by the life span of the Church itself. What is the secret of this life span, the secret of the "days that may be long" of the religious communal orders? It is that they are faithful to the Church as their "mother," and that they strive to fulfill the will of their founders, their "fathers," in accordance with their vows. The secret of their long life span lies in their fulfilling the commandment: *Honor your father and your mother*.

Valentin and Maria Tomberg, in Ährengarben bei Perscheid, Germany, 1966

The Elemental Rosary

Philippa Martyr

HAVE RECENTLY REAL-
ized that the Rosary
restores creation. It is
an elemental prayer,
woven deeply into the
Genesis narrative and the history of
the People of God, first as Synagogue
and then as Church. It goes back into
prelapsarian Eden and runs through it
like the four rivers in the Garden,
merging again into the one river in
Revelations on whose banks are trees
that bear fruit all year round, and in
whose leaves are healing.

I would never have learned this if I
had not struggled with the Rosary all
my life. This meant that I have been
willing to try all sorts of different ways
of sustaining focus. What finally
opened the Rosary for me was the
introduction of the Luminous Mysteries, which I embraced enthusiastically
because I had already been generating
my own mysteries of the Rosary and
praying them.

Since then, the Luminous Mysteries
have become for me a master key for
the other fifteen Mysteries. I have a set
of five alternate names for the five
Luminous Mysteries: the Divine
Nakedness, the Mystical Marriage, the
Planting of the Flag, the Illumination,
and the Body of Christ. As I continue
to try (and fail) to pray the Rosary
daily, it seemed to me that these could
be used as a master key to all twenty

mysteries, and that each corresponds
with an element: water, air, earth, and
fire, with the fifth element of love—
finding that which was lost—combining all four in the final mystery of each
cycle.

The Divine Nakedness
(*Water*)

This is the mystery of beginnings: in
Genesis with the watery creation
under the movement of the Spirit, the
water in the womb in which the baby
grows, the immersion of baptism, the
watering of the ground in the garden
with Jesus's sweat of blood, and
Mary's tears in the garden as she looks
for the buried Jesus. Within each
beginning is the promise of death, but
also of resurrection.

Each first mystery begins a cycle, a
new proto-creative step: the incarnation of the naked Jesus in Mary's
womb under the brooding Spirit; the
plunge of Jesus's body into the Jordan
to open the baptismal font; the first
emotional and physical opening of
Jesus's body in the agony that will give
birth to the Church; and his bursting
forth, naked and resurrected, from the
tomb on the eighth day of creation.
They all involve physical, emotional,
and spiritual nakedness: the nakedness
of that same body of Christ to which
we will return at the end of the cycle.

The Mystical Marriage
(*Air*)

Air comes second in the story of Creation because it parts the waters above the heavens from the waters below. The Book of Revelations tells us that there is no sea in the new creation: the sea separates us into peoples, but there will be no more separation between heaven and earth, or between us.

Each second mystery marks both the separateness and union of heaven and earth in a mystical marriage, with and without words. The visit of Mary to Elizabeth unites the Old and New Testaments, a natural marriage and conception in the Old and a spiritual marriage and conception in the New. Elizabeth and baby John receive the Holy Spirit through the spoken word of Mary. The wedding at Cana celebrates the blessing of human marriage and the divine marriage of the Cross, and the spoken word of Mary to "Do whatever He tells you." During the scourging at the pillar, Jesus atones for the sins of the flesh and sins against marriage in a particular way. Here, there are no words; there cannot be words, but only cries. At the Ascension, heaven and earth meet again in mid-air in the person of the One who ended the war between the two in his own flesh.

The Planting of the Flag
(*Earth*)

Out of the space between air and water arose the earth. The earth was created for Christ; it is his to conquer, and he conquers by planting his standard into it, at the very center of the cycle of five mysteries—through

Adam's skull at Golgotha, and deeper still into the skull of the primal serpent.

Christ comes as conqueror, but in many guises. He comes as a baby, adored as a king, interrupting time and space, disrupting rulers, rearranging the heavens, and reordering the lives of his parents, as all babies must. The beachhead is established, and conquest continues with the proclamation of the Kingdom, bringing food and love. More territory is seized with the crowning with thorns—the breaking of the heart of Jesus on Pilate's balcony drives the flag yet more deeply through his own heart into creation, where he must remain planted forever. Finally, the flag is crowned with fire as the Holy Spirit descends and completes the birth of the Church on earth, where it too will remain until the end of time, spread out across time and space, terrible as an army with banners.

The Illumination
(Fire)

Out of the earth came fire. In the fourth mystery, illumination follows in the wake of the conquest of earth for the Kingdom of Heaven. Fire burns, cleanses, and purifies; it also lights the way in the darkness as it did in the desert for Israel. This is a fire that leads, like a beacon.

In his presentation in the Temple, God himself enters the Temple by the east gate, setting the eyes of his servants aglow. Knowledge follows: Simeon understands, and so does Mary. As Jesus is transfigured, he is set alight; and, in his light, his disciples see themselves for who they really are:

foolish and weak and loving and in need of repentance. In the carrying of the cross to Calvary, followed by the infant Church in the form of his handful of followers, Jesus sees ahead of him not only his death, but his resurrection. As Mary is assumed, she burns like an icon across the heavens and takes her place standing on the crescent moon, where she will be crowned with stars.

The Body of Christ (Love, or the Finding of What Was Lost)

The fifth mystery brings us to the beginning once more in the Body of Christ, which is both the source and summit of our worship, and divinely naked. Love is that element which finds what was lost, and the fifth mysteries all involve loss and finding.

The child Jesus was not lost, but his parents were. Finding him was their journey, rather than his, driven on by love through days and nights. In the Eucharist, the body of Christ is both lost in the species and found in faith, more truly present than the host itself. The crucifixion lost Jesus his life; it bought our salvation, in which he reversed the journey of our first parents and unravelled time and space to atone for our sins. When Mary is crowned, it is because she is the icon of the Church, and the great finder of those that are lost: the finder in the Temple, the giver of her flesh to form his body, and the champion at the standard of the cross where her heart opens to universal spiritual motherhood. She reaps first the reward that we will in turn reap: heaven and earth made whole again.

Saying the Rosary in this way walks us through the entire creation: the nakedness, the marriage, the conquest of the earth, our heavenly illumination as it should have been without the Fall, and the Body of Christ when God comes to live among us. Mary is the wisdom of God; the feminine principle described in the Book of Wisdom, and mother of God. All things—including Creation—can be restored in her through her cooperation with God, because of and through and with the cross and resurrection.

Diotima the Stranger

Andrew Kuiper

HE CHARACTER OF Diotima in Plato's *Symposium* is by far the most evocative figure in the entire Platonic corpus. Despite her brief appearance in this dialogue, she is portrayed as having had a singular influence on the young Socrates. While it is true that the *Parmenides* also portrays a young Socrates, there the dialectical encounter is presented as a single troubling conversation with Zeno and Parmenides that raises thorny questions about the doctrine of the forms. By contrast, in the *Symposium* Socrates alludes to the fact that he had approached Diotima intent on instruction and benefited from her teachings over the course of many conversations. Yet despite the multiple meetings and presumably some intimacy that naturally occurs in teacher-student relationships, he continually refers to her as "the stranger from Mantineia." From the moment she is introduced in the dialogue, she both fascinates and estranges the reader. It would be difficult to exaggerate her importance both to the *Symposium* and to the broader project of Platonic philosophy.

She is entitled, more than any other character, to be called the teacher of Socrates. It would even be appropriate to suggest that Diotima provides a mysterious doubling of the account Socrates gives of his philosophical origins in the *Apology*. Specifically, she provides a very different perspective on why it was that Socrates set out on his philosophical quest in the first place. As is famously known from the *Apology*, Socrates relates that he and his friend Charaephon journeyed to Delphi and were given an Apollonian oracle: *no one is wiser than Socrates.* This divine utterance drives the humble stonemason to an almost feverish pitch of dialectical argumentation attempting to honor the words of Apollo. Socrates plays the gadfly to Athens, in and out of season, because of religious duty. The entire *elenctic* approach of questioning and conceptual clarification is meant to vindicate the gods as Socrates punctures the bombast of unreflective or mendacious interlocutors. Only then can Apollo be proven correct in identifying Socrates, who knows he is not wise, as the only *relatively* wise man. This goes hand in hand with his *daimon*, which is a kind of intermediary spirit and not, as is sometimes falsely implied, the "voice" of his conscience. His *daimon*, however, only ever prompts him in a negative fashion. He is moved by it to either reject facile conclusions or even avoid conversation with persons altogether. In total, the effect of both the Apollonian oracle and the *daimon* are primarily apophatic.

The origins of the Socratic quest that we find in Diotima, however, bring to light something else entirely. While her guidance is not in contradiction to the origin we read about in the *Apology*, she provides the young Socrates with a distinctly positive vision of what purifying dialectic is meant to attain. Her gift is kataphatic in nature. Diotima herself is an extraordinary manifestation of divine power and wisdom. She is presented in almost overwhelming terms as a woman who is equal parts prophetess, priestess, and wonder-worker. Her historicity is taken for granted both in the dialogue and for centuries of reception-history until the writings of Ficino. The abundance of allegorical wealth to be found in her name— *Diotima Mantinike*—was not seen as a disqualifying factor for her concrete existence. "Diotima" means alternatively one who honors or is honored by Zeus and "Mantinike" (or *from Mantineia*) contains the root for prophecy (*mantis*) and victory (*nike*). Her extra-textual existence is not a necessity, but it is pertinent to point out that Mantineia was and is a real city that had an alliance with Sparta against Athens during the time-period of the dialogue. It is also worth noting that in Plato's writings "nearly all his named characters are known to be based on real persons, and the few exceptions are likely to have been real as well."[1] If that is the trend through-

out the dialogues, it would be odd to assume otherwise in this specific instance. But again, even accepting Diotima's relegation to a purely literary entity should not stifle enquiry into the curious case of her existence in the drama and in Plato's thought.

There has been an unfortunate habit among many readers and even scholars of the *Symposium* to flatten Diotima into the role of an exotic mouthpiece for Socrates's own thoughts. There is, of course, a long history of critical suspicion of anything that smacks of myth, mystery, or mysticism in the Platonic corpus. Legions of scholars after Schleiermacher have tried to "save" Plato from these supposed horrors by treating them as decorative rhetoric, sops for the masses, or even as entirely disingenuous. Thankfully, this impoverished prejudice is slowly but surely being overturned by contemporary scholarship. Kneejerk aversion to the religious dimensions of Platonic philosophy, or uncritical acceptance of a severe Platonic/Neoplatonic schism, is no longer the norm. Scholars like Nancy Evans now argue openly that Diotima is not only a prophetess but "like the goddess Demeter . . . a sort of mystagogue, one who initiates individuals into her Mysteries."[2]

Diotima manifests and perfectly unites the three aspects of Platonic philosophy most despised by critical Enlightenment scholarship: thaumaturgy, theurgy, and theosis. It is no wonder that her distinctive role has

---

[1] Ruby Blondell, *The Play of Character in Plato's Dialogues* (Cambridge, UK: Cambridge University Press, 2002), 31.

[2] Nancy Evans, "Diotima and Demeter as Mystagogues in Plato's Symposium," *Hypatia*, vol. 21, no.2, Spring 2006.

been overlooked. Her explicitly religious stance upsets the clear distinction between rational Socratic philosophy and later ostensibly irrational and syncretic corruptions. These skeptics cling to Damascius's offhand comment that for some Platonists philosophy is primary and for others hieratic practice is of first importance. Yet, according to Damascius's own divisions, it is the supposedly *philosophical* and anti-ritualistic Porphyry who writes an entire work on oracles and divination and introduces the Chaldean Oracles as a holy text and revelation. To set up Porphyry and Plotinus as the last "safe haven" of Socratic-Platonic rationalism, is to crudely excise the central religious context of their lives: singing and composing hymns to the gods and celebrating the birthdays of Socrates and Plato as sacred festivals. By Porphyry's own account, Plotinus once praised him for being a "poet, hierophant, and philosopher" all at once for ecstatically composing a mystic poem at one of these occasions.

Whatever Damascius meant by dividing the followers of Plato into different categories, he did not mean some kind of fundamental division between religion and philosophy. And he absolutely did not mean to set up *philosophy* as the kind of activity that could be recognized as genuine under a Cartesian, Humean, or Kantian model. The shrine which Plato himself consecrated to the Muses within the grove of plane-trees at the Academy belies any accusation that he meant religious practice to be something alien to philosophy.

Diotima is a scandal and cause for offense because she reminds scholars that this religious "irrationalism" is nestled in the very heart of the Platonic account. She mocks them and gives them a bad conscience. They remember, even if only for a moment, that Socrates interprets dreams as divine commands (*Phaedo* 60e-61a), is concerned with traditional sacrificial obligations such as a rooster for Asclepius (*Phaedo* 118a), and in a painstakingly clear and public address attributes his philosophical quest to the divine oracle of Delphi—the manifestation of Apollo's will on earth. However, they soon turn away from the mirror that Diotima's witness presents and promptly forget what they saw there.

Socrates introduces his memory of Diotima by calling her, without much preamble, his instructress in the arts of love (*ta erotika*). She had traveled from Mantineia to Athens in order to delay the plague that would famously strike Periclean Athens. Astonishingly, Socrates mentions almost as a passing aside that she was successful in delaying that gruesome catastrophe by a decade! Whether this was through skill in offering sacrifices or by means a direct thaumaturgic act is unclear. Either way, Diotima is immediately established as possessing almost incomprehensible power. How she became his teacher is never explained; however, there are hints that the young Socrates was being assessed or prepared for something to come. The reader immediately notices how flustered the young Socrates is. For readers of Platonic dialogues, the shift from Socrates as a clinical dialectician who dismantles his interlocutors with little effort to a Socrates constantly on the back foot is jarring. At certain moments, he seems almost to plead with Diotima and reproach her for asking too much of him: "If I had known, I should not have wondered at your wisdom, neither should I have come to learn from you about this very matter" (206b).[3] She is often smiling or laughing at the responses of Socrates. In at least one place Diotima actually shushes him: "Hush, she cried" (*ouk euphemeseis* or 'will you not avoid words of ill omen?') (201e). This is not to suggest that her tone is cruel. Diotima evinces genuine interest and even a gentle concern for her pupil at times. Yet, there is a constant and unmistakable undercurrent of authority in the content of her teaching and the manner of her presentation. The young Socrates is being subjected to a kind of purifying examination that is meant to cultivate a reverential attitude. One place that conveys this is when Diotima makes a half-joking comment: "These are the lesser mysteries of love (*ta erotika*) into which even you (*kan su*), Socrates, may enter (*mutheies*)." The banter at Socrates's expense, however, quickly shifts to a more serious tone. Diotima is now clearly speaking of a kind of cultic initiation. "To the greater and more hidden ones (*ta de telea kai epoptika*) which are the crown of these, and to which, if you pursue them in a right spirit they will lead, I know not whether you will be able to attain. But I will do my utmost to inform you, and do you follow if you can" (209e–210a). The good-natured ribbing that Socrates can only enter the lesser mysteries is accompanied by the solemn promise that Diotima intends to prepare him for further sacred revelations to the best of her ability.

As multiple scholars have noted, the terminology of initiation (*mutheies*) and mysteries (*mustika*) is that of the Eleusinian mystery-cult. "Plato's fourth-century audience would have immediately made the connection between Diotima's rites of love (*erotika*) and Demeter's rites of initiation (*mustika*) when they heard Diotima mention her higher grades of initiation (*epoptika*) and their rituals of sight."[4] Evans points out that the word *epoptika* in particular has no known meaning outside its unique association with the Eleusinian mysteries. Even the language of "greater" and "lesser" mysteries has a known cultic equivalent. A candidate participating in the lesser mysteries, held in Athens, would be made one of the *mystai*. The *mystai* at a later date would then walk eleven miles in a festive procession to the city of Eleusis where the greater mysteries, the culmination of the ritual, were manifested in the sacred Telesterion. Diotima's tutelage of Socrates is a promise to lead him in a sacred procession to a culminating vision of divine union. "The encounter with Beauty and Being is depicted as a rite that one can be initiated into as one was initiated into the rites of Demeter at Eleusis."[5]

Though the *Symposium* contains the most prominent instances of this

---

[3] All translations are from *Dialogues of Plato*, trans. Benjamin Jowett (New York, NY: Random House, 1937).

[4] Evans.

[5] Ibid.

terminology, mystery-language is scattered throughout the Platonic corpus (for instance *Phaedrus* 249d). As Gwenaelle Aubry correctly notes "it is not a matter of whether Plato used mystery-language but how."[6] Gwenaelle Aubry and others argue that Plato's mysteric language, while deliberate and prominent, is still ambiguous and somewhat detached. To my mind, this interpretation is too much swayed by the idea that religion would dilute the fundamentally *philosophical* message of Plato. It also fails to account for the fact that union with divinity (*theosis*) was the explicit goal of philosophy both within the Platonic corpus and among the various philosophical academies of ancient philosophy. Diotima makes this explicit in the *Symposium* by saying that the *telos* of philosophy is to behold beauty bare while becoming an immortal (*athanatos*). The one who is god-loved and god-loving (*theophiles*) will conceive and bear the ultimate beautiful realities (212a). The same goal is expressed in a different way in the *Theaetetus*: "Therefore we ought to escape from earth to the dwelling of the gods as quickly as we can; and to escape is to become like god, so far as this is possible" (176a–b). By understanding Diotima and her use of mysteric language in the *Symposium*, we are able to correctly navigate all the religious references in the Platonic corpus whether they be mysteric, mystical, or magical. Put more starkly, Diotima redeems Socrates and Plato

from being opportunistic pilferers of sacred language for secular purposes. Platonic rationalism is a *hyperrationalism* which performs its task underneath alternately solar and nocturnal illuminations. The task of dialectic and conceptual purification can no more be considered opposites to ecstasy and madness than sunlight can be considered the opposite of moonlight and starlight. All of these realities inhabit the same cosmos even if it is difficult for us to perceive their modes of illumination at the same time.

Some however have raised against Diotima's speech the charge of demythologization. By denying that Eros is a god but is instead merely a *daimon* doesn't Diotima naturalize desire? Isn't it also true that Diotima is pitting herself against traditional cosmogonies, like those of Hesiod and Orpheus, where Eros is portrayed as a fundamental world-begetting divinity? The mention of these cosmogonies in an earlier speech by Phaedrus cannot be accidental. Diotima's speech is certainly meant to be read in light of previous speeches in the *Symposium* but here the point is more likely to pressure these traditional mythologies and purify them. Consider Socrates's statement in the *Phaedo* that he would be willing to die many times over if it means meeting Orpheus, Musaeus, Hesiod, and Homer (41a). This effusive outburst in the face of imminent execution suggests that he views these figures in an ultimately positive life. Think also of the fact that later on in this same speech Diotima will praise the poetry of Homer and Hesiod as having acquired immortal fame and being worthy of emulation (209d). The

---

[6] Gwenaelle Aubry "Plato, Plotinus, and Neoplatonism" in *The Cambridge Handbook of Western Mysticism and Esotericism* (Cambridge, UK: Cambridge University Press, 2016).

point is not to overturn these poems but to read them in the way most worthy of the gods. The subtle questions of chaos, desire, and the formation of the world require clarification which is not always provided by narrato-mythological genres. Consider for context the way in which Socrates pointedly questions Agathon on the divinity of Eros and the way in which the young Socrates was chastised concerning this same point. The definition of Eros presumed by Agathon and the young Socrates includes a fundamental lack of fullness; a thirst derived from need and dissatisfaction. If this definition of Eros is allowed to stand and then stand in for divinity, the divine nature becomes more like a hungry envious maw than something worthy of worship. The "limitless sea of beauty" (210d) described by Diotima does not need to be refilled by an external source—though its delight is to diffuse and overflow itself.

Later Platonists and Christian theologians took the distinction *eros* as desire fueled by an ontological lack and *eros* as divine desire to overflow from abundance. The divine does not earn its divinity but creation most fully expresses and makes the Absolute manifest through multiplicity; and even the process by which all creation revert to the One is not a dissolution but a recuperation where all things participate in the divine nature inasmuch as it is possible for them. Plotinus, understanding the different connotations of *eros*, has no objection to applying the latter sense to his highest metaphysical principle: the One beyond Being. In a similar vein, the Christian Neoplatonist (and probably student of Proclus) Pseudo-

Dionysius the Areopagite also argues that *eros* is not only appropriate but perhaps one of the highest names for God. He even goes so far as to suggest it is a more appropriate name than *agape*. This late-antique conclusion about *eros* among Platonists and Christians is not dispositive proof of this interpretation; yet, it is a remarkable consensus. If Plato meant Diotima's speech to decisively decouple *eros* from the highest divinity, it is noteworthy that it utterly failed to effect his most assiduous followers.

The central role the myth of Eros's origin plays in Diotima's speech also undercuts simple ascriptions of "demythologization." The birth of Eros from Poros and Penia on the birthday of Aphrodite is obviously allegorically charged. However, it would be unwarranted to assume that the story is merely metaphysics hastily dressed in narrative garb. Later Platonists, like Iamblichus, Proclus, and Plutarch, expressed sophisticated views of myth which allowed for both critique and reverence. "Just as the rainbow, according to the account of the mathematicians, is a reflection of the sun, and owes its many hues to the withdrawal of our gaze from the sun and our fixing it on the cloud, so the somewhat fanciful accounts here set down are but reflections of some true tale."[7] The festive Olympian setting of Aphrodite's birthday where gods and demi-gods are inebriated with nectar retains its significance when we

---

[7] *Isis and Osiris* 358–59, trans. Frank Babbitt from *Moralia* vol. 5 of the Loeb Classical Library (Cambridge, MA: Harvard University Press, 1936).

approach the scene with this kind of second naiveté. For one thing, this account reverses Pausanius's early description of two Aphrodites. By maintaining that Aphrodite is one goddess and that she is Beauty without any caveats, Diotima undercuts Pausanius's bizarrely misogynistic claim that the heavenly Aphrodite is purely masculine and the corruptible and common Aphrodite is a mixture of masculine and feminine elements. Diotima further dismantles Pausanius's gynophobia and names generation, particularly human generation, as a privileged sign that all things desire immortal beauty. They are "immortal principles in the mortal creature." Years later, Plotinus will echo this claim in his stunning conclusion that all generation is contemplation.[8] The mixture of male and female does not result in a debased and corrupt Aphrodite; it is a profound, though still relative, image of Beauty Herself.

It is also important to point out that when Diotima plays with imagery of pregnancy as a male trait she is upending an overly static tradition of dividing the genders into purely active and passive roles. Pythagoras before Plato and Aristotle after him insisted that maleness should be grouped with unity, light, goodness, activity and other positive attributes in binary opposition to femaleness, multiplicity, darkness, evil, passivity, etc. While we should be very careful in transposing Platonic conceptions of gender into contemporary contexts, both in the *Symposium* in the *Republic* we

encounter far more surprising and complicated views than anything in Greek society or even most Greek philosophy. Wendy Brown, for example, has argued that Plato regularly "engages in a critique of the socially male modes of thinking speaking and acting prevalent in his epoch and milieu."[9] For instance, he deems women capable to be philosophers, warriors, and politicians. We also know that Plato had at least one female student, Axiothea of Philus, who studied at the Academy under Plato and later under Speusippus. The ripples of Diotima's influence can also be seen by another probable female student under Speusippus—Lasthenaeia of *Mantineia*.

The image of pregnancy does even more than complicate the received binary oppositions of gendered activity. The phenomenon of pregnancy and birth, a biologically female and supposedly inferior state, is exalted as the highest analogy for the philosophical life. The agony of desire is only alleviated at the approach of the goddess Beauty (continually and consistently portrayed in mythically feminine terms). Since seeking wisdom means the desire to not only possess and unite Beauty but to give birth to more beauty, the images of pregnancy and fertility are fully sanctioned as divine signs in contradistinction to Pausanius. Evans points out that the idea of birth in beauty should be associated with the Athenian festival of Thesmophoria, which celebrated

---

[8] See *Enneads* III, 8, [30].

[9] Wendy Brown, "Supposing Truth Were A Woman: Plato's Subversion of Masculine Discourse," *Political Theory* 16, no.4 (1988).

Demeter and Kore culminating "in a joyous day called Kalligeneia, the Day of Beautiful Birth."[10]

Diotima does not disagree with Pausanius, however, that Beauty should be identified with Aphrodite, and the myth of Eros's conception on Aphrodite's birthday unites the entire discourse on love and beauty. Aphrodite incites the agony of desire in all things and her approach brings all pregnancies to parturition. She engenders all bodily and spiritual birth (perhaps why Plotinus and Ficino both identified her with the world-soul). And since Diotima is explicit that the goal of philosophy is turning toward unalloyed Beauty, it would not be incorrect to say that the search for wisdom is interchangeable with seeking the goddess Aphrodite.

If Beauty does all this, what remains for Eros to do? If the demythologization of Eros is not Diotima's intent, what follows from calling *eros* one of the great *daimones*? Her description of his tasks and functions are multifaceted to the point of bewildering. It is Eros who transports the prayers and sacrifices of worshippers to the gods; again, it is Eros who communicates divine messages and commands back to mortals. Diotima describes the gods as trapped behind a great chasm and unable to mingle with creatures without the help of intermediaries. Eros seems to be the most prominent of the *daimones* and in some way appears to underlie all divine-human mediation. Since he is neither purely divine nor purely mortal, neither fair nor foul, neither wise

nor foolish, he is a kind hypostasized *betweenness*; he is called a *metaxu* (a term familiar to readers of William Desmond). Signs, symbols, wisdom, and even existence are constantly ebbing and flowing through him, he is constantly dying and being born again. These confounding descriptions of *eros* might be a demotion if we think they are meant to apply to the highest divinity. However, it is obvious that this *daimon* is meant to model the human pursuit of wisdom. As Diotima says, "he is a philosopher at all times" (203d). Taken in that light. Diotima's speech is one that heightens, enchants, and mythologizes the role of the philosopher to an almost staggering degree. They are both semidivine (*to daimonion*). Eros is not limited to an interpretive or communicative function; his powers include the entire gamut of priestly, prophetic, and even magical activities. For "in him all is bound together and through him the arts of the prophet and the priest, their sacrifices (*thusia*) and mysteries (*teletai*) and charms (*goeteia*), and all prophecy (*mantike*) and incantation (*epoidoi*), find their way" (202e–203a). At one point, Diotima even calls Eros a sorcerer (*goeis*). Neither philosophers nor the great *daimon* Eros are gods since they thirst for the manifold ocean of Beauty Herself. Yet their activities, which richly deserve to be described as *hermetic*, help marry heaven and earth in order to produce a transfigured unity.

One tantalizing possibility remains obscured just beyond the horizon of the text: could Diotima be Aphrodite in disguise? Her powers are certainly goddess-like and she seems intimately acquainted with religious mysteries.

---

[10] Evans.

In fact, according to one of the Homeric Hymns, Demeter came in disguise to Eleusis and later showed the inhabitants the rites which became the Eleusinian Mysteries. Diotima seems to know a lot about what happened during Aphrodite's birthday; she even knows enough to correct Hesiod and Orpheus on the origin of Eros. Evans points out that after one of Diotima's cryptic statements, "Socrates is still puzzled, [he] responds by saying that he needs prophecy (*mantineia*, 206b9) . . . to figure out what she is saying."[11] Only oracles require prophetic interpretation and only gods, or goddesses, speak through oracles. Lastly, the continual use of the term *stranger* in referring to her implies that there is a reserve to Diotima that can never be exhausted. No matter how many meetings with her or however long she is in Athens, something remains about her that is *beyond*.

In any case, whether directly or indirectly Diotima does act as an oracle of Aphrodite by expounding the mysteries of love to Socrates. The seeress who highlights "the specifically female activities of giving birth and nurturing" serves as spiritual mother and mystagogue for the hapless young Socrates. Along with Apollo's sign at Delphi, the stranger from Mantinea should be counted as Socrates's other, and equally important, oracular and Olympian origin. The thirst for reality which drove Socrates, Plato, and the entire Platonic tradition owes much to not only Apollo the Light-Bringer, but Aphrodite, *eratotrophus*, the

Mother of Love. Let us then treat Diotima as central, not incidental, to Platonic philosophy and our own efforts to discern the mysteries of eros.

For our contemporaries, Diotima and Plato present a clear challenge: philosophy as a fundamentally religious task. The search for wisdom is grounded not only in the belief in divinity but in a host of intermediary non-human entities. In this conception, revelation as a matter of insight into the cultic mysteries or through reading traditional sacred poems provides the crucial horizon of discourse. Again, this does not mean a simple dichotomy of slavish obedience to authority against emancipated critical reason; for Plato, critical reason works both from this framework and upon it. Modern philosophy, by contrast, has been unable to sustain myth and mystery and so has subsequently failed to sustain a robust account of reason. Analytic philosophy contents itself with endless analyses of moral and logical language-games while simply redescribing current political and social norms. Meanwhile, Continental philosophy gnaws at the bones of leftover sacramental and mysteric terminology to try and fill the religious void without religion. For those calling themselves theologians, there is also a reckoning. By hoarding the realm of mystery and revelation for a specific slate of dogmas, they have allowed the emergence of a reflection that thinks it lives beyond myth and ritual. Like modern versions of Pausanius, they have posited a heavenly Aphrodite (theology) and an earthly (philosophy). They also need to be hushed by Diotima and learn again of the undivided goddess of Beauty and

---

[11] Ibid.

how all wisdom begins with the *ta erotika*. Love is the goal of all our striving and nothing is truly philosophy or a mystery without it. As St. Paul tells us, if we have prophetic power and can fathom all mysteries but have not love, we are nothing.

Diotima persists as an indomitable witness to that Pauline declaration: "faith, hope, and love abide, these three; but the greatest of these is love."[12]

[12] 1 Corinthians 13:13.

DIOTIMA

Bliss of the heavenly Muse who on elements once imposed order,
Come, and for me now assuage the chaos come back in our time,
Temper the furious war with peace-giving, heavenly music
Till in the mortal heart all that's divided unites,
Till the former nature of men, the calm, the majestic,
From our turbulent age rises, restored to its prime.
Living beauty, return to the destitute hearts of the people,
To the banqueting table return, enter the temples once more!
For Diotima lives as do delicate blossoms in winter,
Blessed with a soul of her own, yet needing and seeking the sun.
But the lovelier world, the sun of the spirit is darkened,
Only quarrelling gales rage in an icy bleak night.[13]

[13] Friedrich Hölderlin, *Selected Poems and Fragments*, trans. Michael Hamburger (New York, NY: Penguin Books, 1998).

READING RILKE IN SOUTH CAROLINA

Paul Hunter

The wetland is a great plane,
Smooth green bottle glass,
Solid to bear a man's weight.

Two eyes interrupt the plane.
The advent of the alligator is
Without violence, sound or motion.

How long were they there
Seeing, unseen?
Are they always there?

Behind the eyes a path in the water was
The only token of a history
Of any merciful declension from eternity.

I recall lines from Rilke
That perhaps I do not really understand:

"Beauty is nothing but
The beginning of terror, that we are still able to bear,
And we revere it so, because it calmly disdains
To destroy us. Every Angel is terror."

Is every terror, too, an angel?
Bearing tidings of what, from where?

Terror is the interruption
Of one order by another.

When graves are opened,
Or cracks appear in heaven's crystal spheres,
There is terror.

Beauty is the great interrupter—
That beauty that arrests me
On an afternoon walk in the marsh

When two eyes appear
Without violence or sound,
To undo my solidity.

But what was interrupted?
The glass that was not solid,
The crystal sphere that never turned.

An altogether unreal order,
A taxonomy of terms and lies,
Smooth surfaces, to keep the angels out.

Angels only interrupt
because we have exiled them.
Their order and ours are rightly one;

As, too, the animals
Once were named,
And knew no terror at our hands.

The alligator has interrupted my order
Just as I have interrupted hers.
We are each other's angels.

A Breath of the Power of God

Hidden Images of the Mother in the Development of Holy Spirit Theology

Madonna Sophia Compton

"God tells us, through the mouth of Solomon, that Sophia is the Spirit."

IRENAEUS *Against the Heresies*, 4.20.3

Sacred Dwelling: The Early Link Between Wisdom and Spirit

N THE PAST FEW decades, Sophiology, or the study of the Wisdom books of the Bible, has become an important emergent theology. In a variety of biblical texts, we find that Sophia is a divine Being who orders the cosmos (Eccles 24; Wisdom 7–9); who courts humans (Song of Songs; Eccles.4); who is the intimate of God (Baruch 3 and Wisdom 8: 1–5); who is a guardian from heaven, (Proverbs 8); who acts like God in relationship to Israel (Wisdom 10–11); who reveals God (Wisdom 7–8); whom God sends forth (Eccles: 24:8); and who invites us to learn Wisdom (Proverbs 9). Perhaps more than any other function, Sophia is a heavenly mediator who loves humans and wants them to participate in the life of God; and to accomplish this, she builds a house and takes up residence with them (Proverbs 1:1–6).

It is not surprising that there are a number of different interpretations in Sophiology, about who and what the Wisdom books are attempting to reveal to us. The texts lend themselves to a variety of explanations. The religious historian Jaroslav Pelikan has claimed that the great crisis in Christology and Trinitarian theology in the early Church began with a dispute of Sophia in Proverbs 8: 20–31. "It was necessary in such a definition to clarify whether the Word that God spoke at creation [was] the Logos now present in Jesus."[1] The disputed passage in Proverbs 8:22 is still translated in very different ways, for example, "The Lord created me at the beginning of his work" (Oxford RSV) and "The Lord begot me, the first born of all his ways" (NAB).

---

[1] Jaroslav Pelikan, *Jesus Through the Centuries; Mary Through the Centuries* (New York: History Book Club, 1985), 62.

During the early Church, the meaning and interpretation of "Word" (Logos) and "Wisdom" (Sophia) became the object of intense controversies, as theological speculation about the role of Christ, Wisdom, and the Holy Spirit evolved. The Gnostics developed complicated mythological cosmologies about the Wisdom Woman in the 2nd century, incorporating many of the goddess attributes of the Hellenistic culture within which the Church emerged; but this understanding of Sophia was rejected by the mainstream Christian tradition.[2] Other Church Fathers refused to abandon Sophia to the role of syncretistic goddess or Gnostic heresy. Many of the early Christian Fathers identified Sophia as Christ, assuming that the descriptions of Sophia in the Wisdom literature applied to the incarnated Logos. Through the struggle to deepen its understanding of Sophia, the Spirit, and the Logos, the early Church emerged with a clarified awareness of the Triune God as it began to interpret Scripture in a way that became decidedly Christian.

Because the Greek word for Wisdom is, like the Hebrew *Chokmah*, feminine in gender and imagery; and because the Hebrew word for the Spirit of God in Genesis (*Ruach*), as well as the Aramaic version (*Ruha)*, is also feminine, the identification of Sophia with the Holy Spirit has led, at times in the Christian tradition—both ancient and modern—to imaging the Holy Spirit in feminine descriptive language. Although a tradition eventually did evolve—and became quite popular during the medieval period of the Roman Church—of associating the Holy Spirit as "Spouse" of Mary, this was not a metaphor in the early Church, which principally saw Mary as the "temple" of the Holy Spirit. The Mariologist René Laurentin has commented on the limitations of linking Mary and the Holy Spirit in a spousal way, since the language is dangerously suggestive of pagan myths of human women who were impregnated by male gods.[3] Theologian Sarah Jane Boss has stressed that it is problematic to envision Mary's relationship with God (either with Christ or the Holy Spirit) in nuptial imagery, lest we reify a symbolic motif.[4] In the Eastern Church, Mary is most often spoken of as the 'temple' or *indwelling* of the Holy Spirit, which then becomes a model for all women. In one of his treatises to virgins, alluding to the parable in Matt 25:1, Athanasius exhorts them to remain as pure *temples*: "will he see his temple shining forth from every side? . . . [for] when he sees your lamp unextinguished . . . he makes you worthy of his Spirit."[5] Likewise, in the 3rd-century text called the *Apostolic Didascalis*, the female deaconess was also perceived to be a temple of the Spirit:

---

[2] Leo Lefebure, "The Wisdom of God: Sophia and Christian Theology," *Christian Century* (19 Oct. 1994).

[3] René Laurentin, "Mary and the Holy Spirit," in D. Plunkett (ed.), *The Virgin Mary and the People of God* (Birmingham: Maryvale Institute, 1999), 32–40.

[4] S. J. Boss, *Mary: New Century Theology* (New York: Continuum, 2004), 63.

[5] Athanasius, Ep. Virg. 2.3, 24.

"And the deaconess shall be honored by you as a type of the Holy Spirit." [6]

The understanding of Divine Wisdom bifurcated in the Christian tradition, with part retaining the older Hebraic and Aramaic association (*Ruach, Ruha*) of the feminine Holy Spirit with the Greek Wisdom-Sophia; and part shifting to the association of Wisdom with the masculine Logos (and therefore Christ). Sophia's description of herself in the Greek Septuagint translations of Proverbs 8: 22–31 was seen by some of the very early Fathers (Athenagoras, Hippolytus of Rome, Origen) as referring to God's eternal Logos. For Origen, Christ was identified with Wisdom and this Christ-Sophia was "begotten beyond the limits of any beginning that we can speak of or understand." [7] Irenaeus insisted that the Sophia of Solomon was the Sophia of the Holy Spirit. In Proverbs 8 and Sirach 24, Wisdom/Sophia is a cosmic principle, holding all things together, a connecting link between the world and the Godhead. Wisdom, the mediator, however, establishes a 'dwelling' in Israel—this is evident in both Sirach 24 and in the Wisdom of Solomon, which alludes more to an internal dwelling, as in the sense of the *Shekinah* (the root of which, in Hebrew means "to dwell"). This holy dwelling is connected to *pneuma*—the Spirit of God in us. After Pentecost, the people of God are transformed to the degree that the Spirit of God was found to dwell in them. The Spirit of Wisdom transforms human understanding from within.

Orthodox theologian Sergius Bulgakov has seen in Origen the "beginnings of Sophiology" which is obscured "by his identification of Sophia with Logos, who for Origen is also a demiurge in a certain sense." [8] For Bulgakov, this marks the beginning of subordinationism in patristic thinking about the Trinity, which would continue to have a fateful influence on patristic theology. Likewise, Boris Bobrinskoy, has observed that the first loss of perspective and disequilibrium in Christology and pneumatology occurred with the Trinitarian synthesis of Origen. [9] While Irenaeus developed a pneumatic Christology, Origen's Trinitarian doctrine "places a notoriously one-sided emphasis on the diverse functions of the Logos (Enlightener, Pedagogue etc.) to the detriment of the role of the Spirit, which he limits to the work of sanctification within the Church." [10] He observes that, for Irenaeus, and later the Cappadocians, who wrote many of the early treatises on the Holy Spirit, the movement of salvation is ascension through the Spirit to the Son, and through the Son to the Father. It is through the illuminating activity of the Spirit's Wisdom (present at Pentecost and beyond) that we may contemplate the Light of the Logos, for the Spirit is the necessary condition for contemplation and worship. Basil explains that a saint becomes the "proper *place* of the

---

[6] Didascalia 11.26.4.

[7] *On First Principles* 1.2 1–2.

[8] Sergius Bulgakov, *The Bride of the Lamb*, trans. Boris Jakim (Grand Rapids, MI: Eerdmans. 2002), 15.

[9] Boris Bobrinskoy, in "Indwelling of the Holy Spirit," *Saint Vladimir's Theological Quarterly* 28:1 (1984): 51.

[10] Ibid, 53.

Spirit, because he (sic) offers himself as the dwelling-place of God and is called the Temple of God."[11]

The Temple is one of the Old Testament metaphors which will accrue to Mary, for she is the Dwelling *par excellence* of all the saints in which God will take habitation; in the development of early Mariology, her first title in the early Church is "Theotokos." There are numerous typologies of Mary in the Old Testament which the patristic Fathers attributed to her; however, let us examine the symbolic associations in the Old Testament tradition which prefigured the Holy Spirit in the Christian Trinity.

Old Testament Metaphors for Spirit

There are many Old Testament metaphors for the Spirit, and the elements (wind, fire, water) are prime examples. God uses the winds to send messengers or angels. A literal translation of the quote Psalm 104:4, "You who make messengers of the winds" is that the messengers are angels. Because the Hebrew word for wind is also breath or spirit, these messengers of God were part of God's Spirit or Divine Breath (*Ruach.*) The element of water in Isaiah appears to prefigure the redemptive action of God's Spirit, which is "poured out," making the desert an orchard and bringing peace to the land (Isaiah 32: 15-17). The metaphor of fire is another frequent attribute describing the movement of the Spirit. God was manifest "in the midst of fire" in Deuteronomy 4:12, reminding the Israelites that the voice

of God in the fire was given for them as "evidence of your wisdom and intelligence to the nations" (Deut 4:6). The image of the burning bush (Exodus 3:2) in the form of the angelic Spirit who appeared to Moses will become an attribute of the Mother of God in later homilies in her honor and also in iconography.

Perhaps the most important symbol, and the one we are most familiar with is the bird. The Torah author, through the mouth of Moses, gives thanks to God, singing, "as an eagle incites its nestlings forth by hovering over its brood, so he spread his wings to receive them" (Deut 32:11)). The dove was the harbinger of new life at the end of Noah's sojourn on the waters. The association of the dove with the Theophany waters at the Baptism of Jesus reminds us that the dove which returned to Noah after the flood heralds a new beginning. Bird imagery, perhaps because it is more concrete than the other images we have been exploring, will remain the dominant motif of the Holy Spirit for centuries. It will appear in countless paintings of the Madonna in Renaissance art, where she is often depicted with a turtle-dove, on in icons of the Annunciation, where she is seen with a dove hovering over her head.

In the Jewish Kabbalistic tradition, although God cannot be seen, the Shekinah is the Spirit who was present in the Old Testament tradition. Shekinah was the mouth of Yahweh, speaking to the prophets. In much of the Old Testament, of course, the God Yahweh was obviously not perceived as the Ineffable Source, but as a masculine god. But as the tradition evolved, so did its Spirit. Later on, in

---

[11] Ibid, 57.

the midrashim, and possibly before, this Spirit is distinctly feminine. When the rabbis of the Talmudic period put well-known proclamations into the mouth of the Shekinah, they now took on distinctly motherly form. By the middle ages, the Shekinah was appearing to Jewish mystics, much like apparitions of the Virgin Mary, always in female form. If it is true that this maternal face of God was repressed in the Old Testament, it did not cease to be an active force in the unconscious of its people.

In the New Testament, the Spirit is known by her functions. The Greek word "paraclete" means "advocate, protector, intercessor, or consoler,"[12] which will become normative titles for the Holy Spirit and later for Mary. As paraclete, she will come as a witness, as a spokesperson, as exhorter. She will dwell with the disciples, of all generations. In her function as Paraclete, the Breath of Life will abide with all of us, as She abode with Jesus.

[12] Donald Gelpi, S.J., *The Divine Mother: A Trinitarian Theology of the Holy Spirit* (New York: University Press of America, 1984), 55–56.

Drawing from a vision of the Virgin
Anne Catherine Emmerich

An Encounter, or
"How I Became a Philosopher"

Max Leyf

 EMONIC BIRDS!" I burst out as I heaved myself from my desk and lumbered across the room. A band of magpies had perched askance along the balcony outside, guided by an instinctual strategy to cry havoc with the greatest acoustic advantage. I closed the window with a thud, knowing it was more of a token than a resolution, for the double-pane of glass remained as transparent to their insolent and incessant squawking as it was to the sunlight streaming through it. Returning to my chair, I took my book in hand. The book had remained opened to the 80th page. "*Monadology*" was printed topmost, and immediately subordinate was the heading "Section 16." I began to read:

> *Furthermore, one must concede that perception, and all that depends upon it, are inexplicable on purely mechanical grounds; that is to say, by means of figures and motions.*

The magpies persisted in their strident cries. I redoubled my efforts of concentration, intent on preparing myself for the following day, when I planned to vanquish Professor Francis on the field of argument:

> *Suppose there were a machine, so manufactured as to think, feel, and have perception: it might be imaginatively increased in size (while maintaining the same proportions) so that one might enter into it even as into a mill. That being so, we should, on examining its interior, find only parts which work one upon another, and never anything by which to explain a perception.*

There must be something wrong with this analogy since it is an obvious
    fact that the brain
produces thoughts just like the mill produces flour. That was it: there is no
    mention of flour in
Monadology. The argument held no weighting for the train while I can't
Immanuel from Prussia that borders Russia and Tchaikovsky's swans
    the mighty birds and yet so soft does music
        On my mind alight, so soft,
            why does it alight so soft?…

— — — — — — — — — — — — — — — — — — —

I RAISE THE EYELIDS, which I did not know had fallen. The room is full of light that seems to have no single source. My gaze catches an empty glass on the table near the window. Like a prism, it showers the table with a thousand subtle rays of colour. My head swims and one of the refractions penetrates my eye, filling my mind with momentaneous light. At once I notice a faint and wafting music, as though of voices singing even as they speak. Along the balcony I see a retinue of beings in their trim, arrayed in piebald iridescent cloaks whose faces shine with a strange and inward beauty. I raise myself expecting a sense of heaviness that would ordinarily accompany this deed. To my surprise, elation floods my limbs and they spring to action. With an excellence that nearly outstrips the speed of thought, they hasten to my spirit's bidding and bear me across the room as a cloud on a sprightly wind. I unlatch the door and the visitors address me in seeming unison:

"Hail fellow, from heralds of the vernal goddess, know that Zephyrus bears our Lady hither, your reception she requesting."

Imagining myself to be taken aback by the unexpected announcement, and nevertheless the words proceed as naturally as the rustle of leaves follows the touch of a breeze in spring: "With reverence do I respect her arrival," I responded, each word seeming backwardly to shape the thought that was its cause.

Before my wondering eyes appears a figure with flowing hair like the grain of birch-wood, and eyes like new leaves. "Sophia," I whisper. I continue, suddenly proud: "These seven years I have made myself your disciple, and I am not the worse for it. My mind has been whetted through trial and through study. Today it glitters like a brand as I skewer my opponents in the ring of disputation."
"Dear boy," she says, with words that laugh like light on rippling streams, "remove the bandages from your eyes; the fool alone thinketh himself wise."

I am filled with a rush of shame at my petty conceits. She looks upon me, and from her gaze I feel a swell of pity. "Forgive me," I exclaim, "I have abused your name with literal-mindedness and profaned your altar with idols of dialectic."

"Your repentance is your entry into the shrine of knowledge. The only heart who can look on Wisdom's feature is the one who sees through the eyes with love. By this light alone can mortals read in the Book of Nature."

"Lady I think I am besotted; a swell of happiness gives shape to airy nothings. But still I believe, and have heard it said, 'Love is reason's blindness.'"
"Silly boy, before you never heard nor looked upon the world at all.
Love gives light to your dark unkindness.
Without love's sight, can reason only grope in blindness."
"How then can I know my thoughts do not deceive,
When all I've learned, would counsel disbelieve?"
"Ask not 'How can I know?' but 'How to love.'"
For you cannot love what is false, nor what you cannot conceive.
Wisdom lights the way for love's feathery warmth to land,
And love takes lovely Wisdom by the loving hand."
I reach out my hand and at once I am swept up on a billow of euphoria. Her voice rings through my mind as sunlight through a crystal. She continues:

"Lo! The green grass waxes towards the sun, and the crocus reaches its tender petals for the sky. But truth will pass you by if you attend no further. The grass is the countenance of higher beings, and the blossom is the face of the spirit's mystery. You must not only look on these outsides, but learn to listen inwardly. When you attend with care and reverence, a world of secret music will announce itself. The whole living world will at once resound in sacramental song.

"A tiger-lilly, triumphant, upward-opening and cupped, sounds the joyful blast of trumpets. The angels play on tulips as on flutes. Violets ring like tiny triangles. Poppies sound in soft and plangent keys. But as you listen deeper you will see that these instruments do not sound of their own accord, but attune themselves to celestial harmonies.

>Their music is an echo of the stars above,
>And angelic hierarchies that sing in choirs of love,
>The love that moves the sun and other stars.
>"Behold the birch; its whole form resounds
>With intervals measured by the music of the spheres.
>The tonic rumbles, stern and muffled, in its solid trunk.
>The second sounds about its first furcation where the bulk
>   divides and ramifies.
>The third emerges with the branch and rounds off its major
>   in the bud.
>The fourth sends its keynote through all that's green.
>And the fifth achieves its glory in the shining blossom.
>The sixth opens not from in the tree, but in being seen
>By other beings from without, in parity and complement;
>A bee alighting on the tender-opened couch
>Within the sanctum of the blossom's bower
>Sounds the sixth for a brief ambrosial hour
>The seventh sings of longing and departure, autumn's key
>The octave echoes in the seed, the birth to be.
>"Behold the sylphs that teach the colours to mingle
>And weave the elements with air and light
>Behold the undines that with the ebb and flow
>Of sap, meander in devoted rhythmic tides
>Behold the gnomes, like miners shrewd and quick of wit
>They lay the roots like briny tracks of life
>And lo! Let your glance graze but do not tarry
>On the fleeting forms of streaming fire
>That wend about the withering blossoms
>Reaping warmth from flowers as they fade
>And the shining summer spirits upward bearing
>To where light patiently waits to receive her own.
>Queen of the Elements: now you know the quinta-essentia.
>Before this day, as skies made dark by stormclouds,
>So your eyes were hid by scales of lovelessness

Let them fall and swift depart
For the eye that clear is portal to the heart
Which is love's exaltation and his throne
As heaven's vaulted ceiling to the sun and stars
That dispel the earth her gloomy shroud
So Nature's book is closed up tight
To the one whose eyes covey no light
You see by the same light you consent give
In which you think and feel and also live.
I take my leave, adieu, adieu
For if my form does not depart from you
My sun will never fill your inner sky
My light will never stream forth from your eye."

Her words seemed to lilt and flutter in the spring air. I gasped. At once I began to
weep. May my tears cleanse and wash away my sin and idiocy, and baptise me
into the church of Wisdom and of truth! During the entire encounter, I had
failed to notice that she had been peopling the meadow with flowers with the
substance of her speech. As though in intimated recollection, I beheld every word
as it descended with a flutter to perch as a blossom, like a thousand butterflies
that bind themselves to the green earth. I had failed to see that with the play of
expression over her features as she spoke, she had been colouring the landscape
in infinite gradients of light and shadow. Each creature was a unique prayer to
Wisdom, and I only had to allow my heart to be instructed in this exultation.

I stood on the balcony and looked out on the vibrant field below. The troupe of
magpies had retired to the roof where they now held conference in a forgotten
tongue. Nature was a speech, a symphony, whose every moment had already
transformed into the one to follow. I recalled a line from one of Rilke's letters:
"how all things are in migration." What remained? I could neither match nor cap-
ture abundance of creation. All that remained was to sing praises to the world's
glory in my own poor tongue; to add my small voice to the chorus of gladness. I
was buzzing inwardly with a fluent euphoria as I returned to the open book on
my desk. I chuckled faintly. Perhaps the reader will not be taken aback if I remark
at the childishness with which "the hard problem of consciousness" now
appeared to me. One might as well quibble over how mere syntax could give rise
to a formulation of the problem in the first place. I returned to the balcony, book
in hand, and seated myself against the south-facing wall. I took up a pen and did
not set it down again until I had scribbled out the following modest lines, which
I have transcribed from the margin of my copy of Leibniz's *Monadology*:

Before the world was made I knew her
Her joy was my completion and delight
She was my only muse and inspiration
By her breath the days were numbered
The seasons were her days and nights

For her the depths and heights were sundered
The axis of the world became her spine
To join the Earth and Sky in life divine
On her hair I patterned plays of sunlight
Which sparks and dances on Elysian streams
Her eyes became the sunbeams
Blithe, the world's joy and lumination
For her form, the rolling Earth did I design
And all the trees and grasses fine
Her smile made me think of flowers
And for her soft reposes, I made the bowers
And about her heart demarked the sacred garden
That stretches four full chambers wide
Therein the life of creatures to reside
And flowing thence in rivers out of Arden
Wherein our spirit-selves abide.

Neuroscience, Sophiology, & the Quest for Wholeness

Sam Guzman

 N HIS MAGNUM OPUS *The Master and His Emissary: The Divided Brain and the Making of the Western World*, psychiatrist Iain McGilchrist summarizes decades of research by arguing that the Western world is a product of a pathological imbalance in the hemispheres of the brain. This pathology is at once the source of the West's technological power and mastery over the created world and the fountainhead of untold misery in the form of nihilism, depression, relational breakdown, and anxiety, among other things. The future of humanity, he argues, is in no small part dependent on our ability to recover a healthy balance between the hemispheres of the brain, for we are in danger of losing all that makes us human.

McGilchrist's thesis is founded upon the fact the left and right hemispheres of the brain represent two ways of seeing and interacting with the world. Contrary to the notion that the right brain is the home of creativity and emotion while the left brain is home to logic and reason, McGilchrist discovered that both sides of the brain are involved in these activities. What is unique about them, he argues, is found not in what they do, but in how

they do it. The hemispheres of the brain represent two distinct ways of encountering and seeing the world.

The left hemisphere of the brain is the seat of reductionist, utilitarian functionality. It is narrow, limited, and focused. It seeks to sever objects from their context and to reduce reality to comprehensible and graspable parts. And, indeed, nearly all scientists now agree that the world we experience is *not* the real world, but a simplified representation of it. Studies of animal sensation have discovered entire spectrums of color, sound, and smell that are beyond our capability to detect. The left brain is also competitive and aggressive, focusing on all that is related to bare survival.

The left brain prioritizes *quantity* over *quality*. It is the left brain that enabled human beings to fabricate tools and begin to employ them. It is what allows us to make machines that can traverse great distances rapidly, or build computers to perform tasks in the fraction of the time of our own capabilities. In art, the left brain's way of seeing is best represented by cubists like Picasso. It's way of seeing is raw, disjointed, fragmented—but highly effective at accomplishing tasks.

The right brain, on the other hand, is concerned nearly exclusively with the whole, with the relationships between things. It consists of broad attention, open and aware of its surroundings. It smooths reality and makes it flow into our consciousness in a connected whole. It prioritizes *quality* over *quantity*. It is the seat of intuition and empathy; of meaning and understanding. It is concerned with all that pertains to life. The right hemisphere detects patterns and perceives categories; it sees similarities and unites the variegated fragments of reality into a coherent whole.

The right hemisphere is also connected to emotional expression and relational receptivity, enabling us to see and perceive personhood in other beings. It is also deeply connected to our sense of embodiedness. McGilchrist relates that those who have suffered right hemisphere strokes lose their connection to entire parts of their bodies. Instead of detecting an arm, they detect nothing. The connection of the psyche to the body, then, runs through the right hemisphere. Artistically, the way of seeing the world of the right brain is best typified by the swirling colors of Van Gogh's starry night or the blurred outlines of the Impressionists.

Why does all this matter? Who cares how we attend to the world, whether it be reductionist or relational? Echoing Simone Weil and myriad other phenomenologists on the power of attention, McGilchrist explains:

> Attention is not just another "function" alongside other cognitive functions. Its ontological status is of something prior to functions and even to things. The kind of attention we bring to bear on the world changes the nature of the world we attend to. . . . Attention changes what kind of a thing comes into being for us: in that way it changes the world.[1]

We live, then, in a participatory universe. Contrary to the mythical "neutral observer" of modern science, we can never *not* participate in the world. What we see, the world we encounter, is indelibly linked to our intentionality. The kinds of attention we cultivate shape how the world responds to us. How we attend to the world shapes the kind world that is created.

Considering the Western world's exploitative utilization of the natural world typified by big agriculture and the unleashing of atomic power, the objectifying consumption of persons perpetrated by pornography and abortion, and the near total loss of meaning engendered by the desecration of the sacred seen in mass media and consumerist meccas like Wal-Mart, it is clear that we have been captivated by the power of the left brain's way of seeing.

Indeed, this is exactly what McGilchrist persuasively argues throughout the 462 pages of *The Master and His Emissary,* citing, among other things, brain scans that show that the size of the left hemisphere of the brain is increasing with time. As a result we find ourselves increasingly alienated from ourselves, our bodies, other persons, and indeed, the whole cosmos. Our reality is fragmented, and we find ourselves desperately longing for wholeness.

---

[1] Iain McGilchrist, *The Master and His Emissary: The Divided Brain and the Making of the Western World*, 28.

Duality, Unity, and Reality

The relationship between these two hemispheres of the brain is nothing entirely new. It is simply one more way of articulating what philosophers and sages have known since antiquity: the world exists of dualities, of polarities that must be balanced and fruitfully united in a creative marriage. In this marriage of opposites lies the wholeness, and holiness, of the human person, and indeed the life of the cosmos.

The brain's hemispheric duality corresponds uncannily to the dichotomy between order and chaos, anima and animus, or the Aether and Chaos of the ancient Greeks. These poles of existence have traditionally been represented as Masculine and Feminine.

The Masculine principle represents stability and utility, the active, the known and the predictable. The Feminine principle represents possibility and creativity, the passive, the new and unknown. Masculine is the Logos, the structuring and ordering principle of all things. Feminine is the Hebrew *ruah*, the maternal spirit of God hovering over the chaos of the unformed world in Genesis. These are two poles of existence whose marriage brings forth the universe as we know it.

Fr. Bede Griffiths, the Benedictine monk and mystic who spent the latter part of his life living in a Christian ashram in India, spoke of these constituent principles of reality:

> There is the physical aspect of matter (*prakriti*), the feminine principle, from which everything evolves, and consciousness (*purusha*) the masculine principle of reason and order in the universe. These correspond to the Yin and Yang of Chinese tradition and the matter and form of Aristotle. . . . In the Vedic tradition the two principles were conceived as heaven and earth, and the whole creation came into being through their marriage.

> These two principles, which are to be found in all ancient philosophy, are no less fundamental in Christian doctrine. St Thomas Aquinas, who built up his system of philosophy on the basis of Aristotle, regarded the "form" and the "matter" of Aristotle as the basic principles of nature. Matter according to this philosophy is pure "potentiality," form is the principle of actuality. . . . Matter as we know it is a combination of form and matter, or of act and potency.[2]

The world that we experience, then, is quite literally born of the conjunction of opposites: the union of potentiality, or Feminine chaos, and actuality, or Masculine order.

But in the Western world, we have forgotten this. We have lost sight of this polarity and necessary marriage of opposites that underlies reality. Dominated by the mascline-left brained way of seeing, we have objectified the world and decontextualized it, reducing it into so many fragmented parts. We have made the world a lifeless and flattened caricature of a rich and textured whole. A world that was once a community of beings has been reduced to an impersonal repository of "natural resources" to be extracted and exploited to

[2] *The One Light*, 58.

achieve desires manipulated by a relentless torrent of advertising.

The Masculine principle of mastery and control at the expense of love, goodness, beauty, relationship, meaning, and morality has all but consumed us, and the results have been devastating. Untold ecological destruction, the pornification and commoditization of human beings, the loss of all natural affection between parents and children—these are but a few sacrifices made on the altar of left-brained consumeristic utilitarianism.

Sophiology and the Recovery of Wholeness

How can the West begin to heal its pathological dominance of the left hemisphere's way of seeing? How can we begin to transcend our reductionist, exploitative, materialistic thinking? How can we learn new ways of attending? Where then, lies our hope?

Simply, we must seek reintegration and wholeness. We must find again intuition, connectedness, relationship, and meaning. We must rediscover all that is common to *life* and not mere mechanism. In neurological terms, we must restore the right hemisphere of the brain's way of seeing and bring our way of encountering the world back into balance.

Throughout his writings, Fr. Bede Griffiths expresses the urgency of this task:

> In the West today, the masculine aspect, the rational, active, aggressive power of the mind, is dominant, while in the East the feminine aspect, the intuitive, passive, sympathetic power of the mind, is dominant. The future of the world depends on the "marriage" of these two minds, the conscious and the unconscious, the rational and the intuitive, the active and the passive.[3]

McGilchrist agrees. Summarizing decades of research, he articulates a possible path towards wholeness:

> If the left hemisphere vision predominates, its world becomes denatured. Then the left hemisphere senses that something is wrong, something lacking—nothing less than life, in fact. It tries to make its productions live again by appealing to what it sees as the attributes of a living thing: novelty, excitement, stimulation. It is the faculty of imagination, however, which comes into being between the two hemispheres, which enables us to take things back from the world of the left hemisphere and make them live again in the right. It is in this way, not by meretricious novelty, that things are made truly new once again.[4]

Imagination, then, is one way to achieve reintegration. Imagination is nothing other than the union of the creative power of the human being with the actuality of the world. The imaginative mind, at once receptive and creative, communes with what is real, feeds on it, and synthesizing it with the unseen ideal, creates that which does not yet exist. One could even say that the imaginal realm is the feminine womb where the union of Aristotle's matter and form are united

[3] Bede Griffiths, *Essential Writings*, 77.
[4] Ibid., 199.

and a new world is conceived. It is the birthplace of a new world.

Imagination could also be seen as the *ajna* chakra of Hindu metaphysics, the third eye or seat of intuitive, holistic seeing. Interestingly, the ajna chakra has in recent times been associated with the pineal gland, seated immediately between both hemispheres of the brain, the uniting link between them.

The path to healing, to wholeness, then, is clear. It is nothing less than a reintegrated form of consciousness, a holistic way of seeing that "marries" the masculine and the feminine, the left-brain and the right brain. Dominated by the masculine, the West must rediscover the feminine and all that it represents. When we begin to do so, we realize that the feminine is not just an abstract principle, but a person. She has a name and a face.

And who is this eternal feminine? None other than Sancta Sophia, the Holy Wisdom of God, after whom Solomon and all the wise men of the ancient world thirsted. She is a mystery that can only be fully learned and proven by experience, but within her are the secrets of life. "She is a breath of the power of God," Solomon tells us, "pure emanation of the glory of the Almighty; so nothing impure can find its way into her. For she is a reflection of the eternal light, untarnished mirror of God's active power, and image of his goodness" (Wis 7:26).

To heal, then, the pathology afflicting us, we must find again the Divine Feminine, Holy Wisdom. We must search relentlessly for holy Sophia, for she will lead us to the water of life. She will teach us to see again the world not merely as an object, but as a sub-ject, filled not with dead matter, but vivified and permeated with the presence and the glory of the Lord. And the task of finding her could not be more urgent. For in the words of Sophia herself, "Whoever finds me finds life. . . . But he who fails to find me harms himself; all who hate me love death" (Prov 8:35–26). Many powerful forces, both seen and unseen, would dissuade us from the path of Wisdom. Death and life are placed before us. We must choose.

Discovering Sophia is not the work of an instant. She tests and proves all those who seek after her. But finding her is finding the way of eternal Life, for ourselves and the whole world. What will occur when we find this Holy Sophia, this eternal feminine? Once again, Fr. Bede Griffiths describes the effects of reintegration:

> The rational mind enters into communion with the intuitive mind, and humankind and nature are "married." The male ceases to dominate the female or to be seduced by her, and a marriage of equals takes place. Both the man and the woman are made whole by marriage. The objective world is no longer an enemy to be subdued but a partner in marriage. There is a saying in one of the apocryphal Gospels: "When will the kingdom of God come?" And the answer is given: "When the two shall be one, when that which is without is as that which is within, and the male and the female shall be one." This is the return to Paradise, the reversal of the effects of the fall.[5]

---

[5] Ibid, 83.

The Western world is on a perilous trajectory. Dominated as it is by the left-brain, masculine principle, it finds itself bound in an endless cycle of warfare, fierce competition, ecological destruction, reductionist scientism, and toxic dehumanization. But there is a way out. Reason must be wedded to intuition, aggression must be tempered by compassion, competition must become cooperation, and scientific discovery must be harmonized with reverence and love. For when the Man and the Woman, the Male and the Female, Adam and Eve are united, then will come the fruitful and joyous marriage feast of eternity.

Abraham's Oak

A Canticle to the Great Mother of God

William Everson
(Brother Antonius, 1912–1994)

"Now all good things came to me together with her, and innumerable riches through her hands, and I rejoiced in all these; for this wisdom went before me, and I knew not that she was the mother of them all. Which I have learned without guile, and communicate without envy, and her riches I hide not."

THE BOOK OF WISDOM

 DREAM I am on a hill overlooking San Francisco. I stand to the east across the bay, the light falling forward out of the west and north as it does toward sunset in summer. I see the merging lines of traffic, usually reminiscent of scurrying ant trails, but now transforming into processions, perhaps religious processions in solemn chant intent upon the source of their life and vitality, slowly descending from the long bridges and the winding freeways beneath me, out of the latency of the darkening world behind. At last I see the outline of the city recede, until in its place only a sublime presence persists, a mysterious feminine implication, evocative and potent, like the memory of the Beloved, evading definition or the strictness of analysis, but haunting and omnipresent. Across the void of that awareness one gull, white-bodied and agile, wheels toward the sinking sun. In the coming of the night, touched by a perfect peace, I stand a long time until, far out in the Pacific, the light drops, and on the darkened west the crescent moon emerges. Then I go down, but neither the crash of traffic, nor the threat of whatever predatory violence menaces the slums through which I wander, can dispel from my mind the reality of that moment, which persists, like a permanent bestowal, and which, I cannot doubt, will change my life forever.

Sometimes I dream you measured of bright walls, stepped on a hill
    and diademed with rose,
Sea-cinctured, the black wave-haunted wharves radialed round your
    hems, and the nuzzling tugs
Shunted like suckling spaniels at your piers.

All the resplendent bridges of your bays converge upon your heart to
    there deploy,

Dilated into streets, fanned to the outmost sectors, bloodlines of pulsant
    use that throbbing flow,
Serving the induct of all crafts and hallowed skills.

Trending into your colonnades at dawn, down from those airgirthed
    arches of the sky,
We pause in tremble, sleep-cozened but reprieved, stirred to the richening
    diastole.
Soaring on noon we sense it loudly replete, swelled to the stately tempo,
    augmented to the day-drummed dance,
Pace of the proudness, an opulence subsumed, the strident fluting and
    the resonance of blare.
Sinking toward dusk we drink a slowed, more moded music, muted, a
    hushed convergence, a deep relapsed repose.
In all the hinterlands about the trains come nosing home, mallowed of
    late light,
Shrilling their long crescendos, creaming with racing lamps the fast
    in-gathered gloom.
Night is your nuance. Listening we hear the wild seabirds, flittered like
    intuition through your coolest thought,
Falter and then fly on, seeding steep sky, the beacon-raftered verge,
South-sought, mewling one plaintive meed, a tremulance of plight,
    before they pass,
Reflashing on pale tips the birth-reverted instinct of all trek.

Hidden within the furlongs of those deeps, your fiery virtue impregnates
    the sky, irradiant with wisdom.
You are Byzantium, domed awesomeness, the golden-ruddy richness
    of rare climes, great masterwork of God.
Kneeling within thy moskey naves, seized in the luminous indult of
    those dusks,
We hold the modal increase, subsumed in chant, ransomed of the balsam
    and the myrrh.
Keeping an inmost essence, an invitational letting that never wholly
    spends, but solemnly recedes,
You pause, you hover, virtue indemnable, at last made still, a synthesis
    unprobed.
Checked there, we tremble on the brink, we dream the venue of those
    everlapsing deeps.

But always there is a somethingness eludes us, Mother, city and citadel,
Proud battlement and spire, croft, granary, and the cool, sky-thirsting
    towers.
Obscure behind those nodes, those many-mingled lights, that wink and
    then well up,

Pale opals on the movement of your breasts, or the navel-cuspèd moon-
    stone at your womb,
Always your essence hovers. The flashing glances of the sea belt you about
    with brightness, blind our eyes,
And the famished senses swoon of that vaunted spicery.

For how could we ever know you wholly as you are, thou who are clearly
    here so manifest of God?
Our coarseness keeps us pinioned of our nerves, while you, immaculate,
    conceived simplicity,
Subsume the inviolable instance. We are unworth, who shunt in stupor
    whelming at your breasts,
Rude shoulderers who sully what we seek, foul our sole good.

But you, that which you have, you give, and give it graced, not as it is but
    as we use it of you,
Dimensioned down to our foreboded taste, our thirst of need, filtered to
    our mereness and our plight.
We suck through sin. Our boon is that you are subsistent of the light,
    bringing the Light to us, whose darkness dams out grace.
Confirmed unto the kindness, gaped mouths of thirst, we tongue a milk
    like honey,
And know from whence it sprung, being yours, who never could taste the
    heaven-nurtured nectar that you use.

Believe us when we seek, Mother and Mercy, who in our lives are
    unbelievable,
All faithlessness of the flesh wrought flaccid, the stunt will burdened in
    the bone.
That need we nurse is sharper than our cry.
Through you alone, the Wisdom and the Womb, keen-creeps the child,
The visionary life fast-set against the acrid element, deaths factual zone.

Clearly you are to us as God, who bring God to us.
Not otherwise than of those arms does grace emerge, blessing our birth-
    blank brow.
Wombed of earth's wildness, flank darked and void, we have been healed
    in light,
Traced to the sweet mutation of those hands, a touch closing the anguish-
    actual stripe,
Whip-flashed the sin, lip-festered on our soul.

This is all plain. But plainness drowns in everything you are, the presence
    you proclaim,
That mystery in which achieves all you are meant.

Squinting our eyes we cannot comprehend.
You we behold, but never what makes you be, the Allness you relate to,
The Finalness you keep, and which we ache to touch.
This thing neither can you say, because of us, lacking your whole capacity
    to know.

But see: out of this too redounds your deepest motherhood;
As one unable to yield the child that utterness no child can spell,
She yet *subsumes* the truth, is the grave wisdom of her wakeful eyes.
Or else the child, callow-stumped and closed, never grows up to what deep
    knowledge is, completes its mode.
Our spirits, watchful, tenacious on their term, see to it only as it gleams in
    you, because of what you are,
The radiance on which the world's blunt might is closed, sharp in a
    singleness simple as any star,
Bright-bought, sheer as one nexus-seeding coal.

Hive of the honey, city and citadel, cathedral and cloister and the cool
    conventual keeps,
Receive us in. The anchorhold of heaven helms us on.
Hungered of that pledge we trample up the ramps limned of a vision,
Questing for what you smile of veiled in rapture mirrored in your eyes,
A solace deeper you said than all such clustered balms,
Pierced to a presence totaled on all truth, vaster than the Prophet's dream
    descried,
And larger, if we believe you, even than your love.

BOOK REVIEW

*The Riddle of the Sophia
and Other Essays*

by John O'Meara (2020)

Kent Anhari

IN 1918's *The Decline of the West,* Oswald Spengler, singular German polymath and prophet of the Second World War, writes of the coming millennium: "to Dostoyevski's Christianity will the next thousand years belong." Russian culture, as Spengler's Goethean study of the shape of history led him to believe, has long been subject to a kind of geological "pseudomorphosis" beneath the pressure of European civilization. While appearing outwardly Faustian, machine-oriented, and urbane, the sublimated current of Russian civilization proper lies dormant, only to achieve full flower in the centuries to come. Spengler's treatment of Russian Christianity is, like many of *Decline*'s rivulets and tributaries, gnomic and dark. It is stirring and suggestive, but fragmentary. Tolstoi and Dostoevski are here "beginning and end clashing together"—Tolstoi the fruit of a mature (even decadent) European, cosmopolitan world and Dostoevski a foretoken of the vigorous Russian soul to come. Tolstoi represents "the last dishonouring of the metaphysical by the social," for whom life is nothing but an exercise in problem-solving, and who can see only Marx when he looks to Christ. Dostoevski, the new metaphysician, "does not even know what a problem is," and, in looking out on the world, sees nothing *but* Christ. In the waning days of Western machine-civilization, only the coming "Christianity of Dostoevski" will be fertile ground for metaphysical and poetic renewal.

It's little surprise that Spengler should harbor such affection for Dostoevski. If anything is typical of Dostoevski and his intellectual peers, it is a Goethean intuition that the parts are justified and made meaningful in reference to the whole of things, and an antecedent attempt to apprehend—to *really see*—the shape of things altogether. Furthermore, it is a faith that the abyss at the heart of Creation, and most especially that of the vexed and burdened human subject, is really luminous with Christ's own light. It has been just this faith in the possibility of a theophoric Creation that has made Russian Orthodox Christianity a harbor of spiritual nourishment and refreshment for many (myself very much included) in the post-Soviet and post-Protestant worlds alike. It is also, ultimately, a Sophiological conviction, and while the core institutional personalities of Pavel Florensky and Sergius Bulgakov are well-researched in Orthodox circles, there remains a more comprehensive story to be told about Russian Christianity which ties the wilder and more distant threads of the Sophiological tradition—back, yes, to Dostoevski and Solovyov and forward to Tomberg and his milieu—into its tapestry. In telling such a broad story, we might make out a clearer picture of the capacious, civilizational and world-historical Russian Christianity glimpsed only obscurely by the likes of Spengler.

In this spirit, I am always grateful for the engagement of thinkers outside of the Orthodox tradition with its intellectual and spiritual heritage, and especially for any attention paid to the filaments which connect the institutional center of the tradition to its peripheries and neighbors. Inevitably, some of the most valuable contributors to such a picture will themselves be of the wilder-and-woolier sort. Such is the case with John O'Meara and his recent work *The Riddle of the Sophia and Other Essays*, an uneven but worthy anthology of Sophiological reflections which enthusiastically joins the speculative, poetical, and practical, and which fits the familiar figures of the Russian Sophiological tradition into a much broader spiritual community. Despite a certain unwieldiness, and the limitations imposed by certain of its assumptions, it is a sincere and earnest work, and one which demonstrates the breadth of territory, both conceptual and practical, which the Sophiological vision makes available.

In O'Meara, we have a guide from that eclectic breed I have elsewhere called "outsider scholars": polymathic in a way that hardly any institutional scholars today can be, independently prodigious in a way that few could imagine being, and possessed of a definite world-picture distinctly his own. With O'Meara, we dive headlong and with little in the way of preparatory or structuring remarks into exegesis. Sometimes this feels like accompanying its author on the journey of discovery, while at others it feels a bit like being crowded in, blindsided, or led through a labyrinth. Enthusiasm and sincerity cover a multitude of sins, however, and for the most part they are sufficient to buoy a reader along to

his next destination until such a time as the itinerary becomes more-or-less clear. His essays, strung together like beads, amount in the final tallying to an overarching investigation into the riddle of Holy Wisdom's coinherence with a world fallen and benighted by folly. Each engages playfully with the structural contours of particular texts while leaving lacunae for the subsequent essays to fill, each advancing its investigation further.

It is to O'Meara's credit that his methodology as an essayist seems as much informed by Sophiological conviction as his subject matter. These are, ultimately, works of literary criticism: tinkering alchemically with the internal matter of this or that text, or else enclosing two or three texts together within a hermeneutical crucible until interesting, even spectacular transformations and revelations take place. They are, like all worthwhile literary criticism, the product of trained and attentive reading. They are also, however, the product of a sincere Sophiological frame of mind: a heartfelt expectation that things really do cohere, and that faithful attention really does disclose luminous spiritual depth.

I will admit, at the outset, that several of these essays will find more ready and receptive readers in those who share both O'Meara's training and his Anthroposophical commitments. Reading *The Riddle of the Sophia* with my own commitments and my own interest in the broader Russian Sophiological tradition, however, I can attest that much of this work demonstrates readily the real fruits that this kind of faithful attention can bear. The collection's first essay, "The Seven Chakras and the Seven I AMs" begins with some quite inspired exegesis of Valentin Tomberg's *Meditations on the Tarot*, involving reconfigurations of Tomberg's own table of correspondences between the "I am" statements of Christ in St. John's Gospel, the Vedic chakras, and the Arcana of the Tarot. O'Meara rearranges the table according to their order in the Gospel in order to arrive at a sequence of spiritual development which he then compares with those of Steiner and Novalis. The account of Novalis's own sequence includes some especially poignant remarks on sickness and death, proposing a perfection of which imperfection must be a part, one "only grasped in a necessary relation to the imperfect." "Through imperfection one becomes open to the influence of others—and this influence of others is the purpose." This is our first indication of this anthology's overriding concern with this question, and one of the very fine ways of broaching it engaged by O'Meara.

The equally ingenious "Sophia and the God in the Flood" pairs Sophia's cries of travail as described in the Gnostic *Pistis Sophia* with closely-matched passages from the Psalms (an exegetical practice, one might note, with an unimpeachably traditional pedigree, but one which is rarely accomplished so effectively) and scaffolds them with reflections from Jung's *Alchemical Studies*. "Like David," he suggests, the alchemist tries "in the midst of his engagement with the material world to release the god within himself who was linked to Sophia," painting an illuminating

fractal-like picture of spiritual restoration undertaken at each level of reality. Urgent for O'Meara in all of these investigations is probing the mystery of fallen nature's relationship to God. He here distinguishes between "Gnostic" and "Hermetic-alchemical" accounts: the former taking the familiar dualist tack, and the latter proposing a much subtler and more interesting sort of theodicy. On the Hermetic account, says O'Meara, the metaphysical priority of Wisdom over the turbid darkness from which she must be liberated makes this darkness a kind of medium for her disclosure: she is "the light *of* the darkness itself" rather than merely its prisoner.

This distinction leads directly onward to a thrilling and illuminating investigation into the cosmogonic writings of Vladimir Solovyov. Solovyov's God, who "desires that *all be* God," fills up nonbeing with Himself in the act of Creation. Insisting that nothing outside of God can be possessed of "autonomous being, a real and positive existence," Solovyov characterizes the Creation as a kind of encounter of the Sophianic World Soul—in which we are, in some sense, commingled—with Chaos. From this encounter, the World Soul (and we with it) will, in the fullness of things, choose God over turbid Chaos and be redeemed. O'Meara's gleanings remind one immediately of the nondualism of the Traditionalist school, and of the cosmogony of René Guénon addressed most probingly and urgently in early essays like *The Demiurge*. Guénon, like Solovyov, stridently and steadfastly withholds from evil the status of a "second principle" which might impugn God's position as sole-existent ground of being, even at the cost of certain classical theological formulae. Given Guénon's role in ushering many in North America, most famously Fr. Seraphim Rose, toward the Russian Church, and the tremendous influence Solovyov had upon the shape of 20th century Orthodox theology in the West, these parallels will be of great interest to readers positioned anywhere in this web of influence. O'Meara notes in Solovyov a certain reticence to take evil seriously enough to address the real encounter with it required of sincere aspirants, and points to a lacuna of practical considerations in this account.

The matter of spiritual practice will be taken up, in part, by Pavel Florensky, as recounted in "On the Sophia in Her Relation to the Creation, and the Further Question of Her Personhood." Florensky offers an ascetic practice which consists not, principally, in a turn *away* from created nature, but toward it—to a practice of attention which draws one out of oneself and forth into the luminous depth of the Creation which is also in God. The second half of the essay is burdened by a lack of appreciation for the robust and somewhat peculiar sense in which Florensky and Bulgakov intend "hypostasis," relying on a common-sense definition of "personhood" to indicate Sophia's implicit (but decidedly glossed-over) status as a distinct divine Person in their work, and in the work of Tomberg and Steiner. This is an exegetical mistake, and one which leads him to suggest that Florensky and Bulgakov were "held back" from saying what they might otherwise have said "by the constraints of theological dogma," a habit of reading which I regard as always uncharitable and, for O'Meara, uncharacteristically inattentive to the peculiar contours of the texts themselves. Nonetheless, there are many worthwhile insights here drawn out of these writers and joined to the work's broader tapestry.

The final essay, and the collection's practical and personal crown jewel, is "Valentin Tomberg and Dostoevski." Here O'Meara addresses Tomberg's invective against Dostoevski in his Letter on the XVth Arcanum of the Tarot. In it, Dostoevski is accused of an overeager and overly-intimate engagement with evil. Several of the threads drawn out in the preceding investigations into the relationship between evil and sanctity, turbidity, and wisdom, here terminate in this most interesting collision between Dostoevski and Tomberg. We have, as in Spengler, another sort of encounter between a terminal figure and an inaugural one: Dostoevski here also representative of a nascent and embryonic Russian spirituality, but one vulnerable to the intoxicating and overwhelming psychological reality of evil which was so potent at the historical turning point from which he wrote, and Tomberg the new Sophiological dawn. Dostoevski feels—*perceives*—intensely the anti-Sophiological logic inherent in the characteristic revolutionary sentiment in his day, which had abandoned the speculative denial of God and had turned to a practical denial of Creation. He understands intimately its effect on the human subject, since he himself has been under its sway. In Dostoevski, Sophiological abundance had not *quite* yet triumphed over Manichaean anxiety, and the worlds disclosed in his novels bespeak lingering doubts about whether the abyss really *can* be luminous. A thorough study of Dostoevski in conversation most significantly with Camus demonstrates a certain therapeutic value in Dostoevski for those not yet weaned off of nihilism. He offers an exercise in pursuing the modern existential condition to its terminus, and to the realization of its unsustainability. This is, like the alchemical descent into Chaos, a dangerous encounter. It is also, for many of us, the only way through.

I express, once again, my real gratitude to John O'Meara for his contributions in this volume, and especially those which engage creatively and freely with the margins of the Russian tradition. They produce some convincing demonstrations of the fact that his tradition's principal strength lies in a new kind of theodicy—a way of making our way through a world vexed by evil which is not only speculative, but poetical and perceptual, borne out of a real and searching encounter with the luminous abyss at the heart of things. Both as philosophy and as the products of practical contemplation, they also demonstrate how credible such a theodicy can be. This is encouragement which we, often overwhelmed as we are by the present darkness, very much need.

PRAYER: DIVINE FEMININE SPIRIT

Lucinda M. Vardey

Divine Feminine Spirit,
Who dwells in our stillness,
Reveal yourself within
So we can bring forth your loving grace.
We celebrate your patience,
We honour your life-giving force
And we hear your call for change.
With your vital power move us to love in action.
With your divine flame ignite us to work for a
        kinder, gentler world of peace.
May your wisdom guide us to know you,
And give us the courage to live your truth.

Contributors

Kent Anhari is an Orthodox Christian from Baltimore, MD, where he lives with his wife, Caroline. His work has been published in *The New Atlantis* and *First Things*.

Madonna Sophia Compton, M.A. Religious History, is a retired professor of Philosophy and Religion, with a deep interest in ecumenical studies, particularly between Orthodoxy and the Anglican tradition. She is the author of *Women Saints*, *Sergius Bulgakov and the Patristic Roots of a Feminine Spirit*, and an ongoing series called *Meditations with...* She is a member of the Episcopal Order of St. Julian of Norwich.

Stephane Gaulin-Brown is an architectural designer and artist based in Montreal, Canada. Following a spiritual emergency in 2015, Stephane pursued a Master's of architecture where he researched potential ways for healing the Modern perception of space as a mere geometric void. Since completing this research, he has been creating a body of work that attempts to attune perception to a view of space beyond mute materialism.

Tyler DeLong is an artist focusing on fine woodworking, carving, print work, and writing. His poetry and block prints have been published in previous volumes of *Jesus the Imagination: A Journal of Spiritual Revolution*. For his day job, Tyler is the director of a skills center, teaching woodworking, permaculture, and wilderness skills for adolescents and families who have experienced trauma. Tyler and his family have a small homestead and workshop in the village of Mechanicsburg in rural Ohio. They participate in the community at St. Paul the Apostle Orthodox Christian Church.

Paul Hunter is an Episcopal priest, living with his family in the low country of South Carolina, where he teaches classical languages and literature at a Christian school. His poetry has appeared in *Jesus the Imagination*.

Andrew Kuiper lives in Hillsdale, Michigan with his wife and three children. He has been published in *The Regensburg Forum*, *Touchstone Magazine*, *The Imaginative Conservative*, *Tradinista!*, *Church Life Journal*, *Jesus the Imagination*, *Macrina Magazine* and *The Lamp*. He is the main contributor to the online theological blog at publishing company *Ex Fontibus* and co-editor of a volume of Nicholas of Cusa translations (forthcoming Notre Dame University Press).

Max Leyf is a Rolfer, philosopher, and anthroposopher from Anchorage, Alaska. He currently balances his time between his Rolfing practice called "The Way of the Elbow" and his teaching responsibilities with Alaska Pacific University. He has published several books, the most recent of which is *The Redemption of Thinking: A Study in Truth, Meaning, and the Evolution of Consciousness*.

Philippa Martyr is an academic, researcher, writer, and student. She lives in Perth, Western Australia.

Alison Milbank is an Anglican Priest and Canon Theologian of Southwell Minster. She is also Professor of Theology and Literature at the University of Nottingham. Her most recent book is *God and the Gothic: Religion, Romance and Realism in the English Literary Tradition* (Oxford University Press, 2019) and she is working on a genealogy of divine immanence in Anglican natural philosophy and poetry.

John Milbank is Professor Emeritus of Religion, Politics and Ethics at the University of Nottingham. He is the author of several books, including *Theology and Social Theory*, *Being Reconciled*, and *Beyond Secular Order*.

Daniel Nicholas is an M. Ed. student in Waldorf Education at Antioch University New England, and holds a B.A. in philosophy from Eastern University near Philadelphia, PA. A teacher by trade, Daniel has taught various subjects at the college and high school levels, including Greek, history, and literature. He is currently a third grade teacher in Oregon.

Michael Sauter is the Retreat House Manager at the Trappist Abbey of the Genesee in upstate New York. He also serves as Director of Catholic Campus Ministry at SUNY Geneseo.

Harpist, singer, composer, educator, and clinician **Therese Schroeder-Sheker** has maintained dual careers in classical music and end-of-life care. She founded the palliative medical modality of music-thanatology and its flagship organization The Chalice of Repose Project. Therese made her Carnegie Hall debut in 1980, recorded for American and European labels, and publishes frequently on contemplative musicianship, music in medicine, and the women mystics.

Valentin Tomberg (1900–1973) was a major Christian Hermeticist, whose anonymously written *Meditations on the Tarot: A Journey into Christian Hermeticism* has become a universally recognized classic. Angelico Press recently published his *The Art of the Good: On the Regeneration of Fallen Justice*, and is preparing several other volumes of his works for publication in the near future.

Miguel Escobar Torres is a Spanish philosopher who works as Professor of Metaphysics, Theory of Knowledge, and Ethics in the Rey Juan Carlos University, in Madrid (Spain). His areas of expertise are medieval philosophy, Byzantine and Slavic thought, mysticism, and Catholic metaphysics.

Although **Bill Trusiewicz** is an inveterate student with wide interests, a love of beauty, and experience and observation of LIFE are his primary teachers. On this basis he writes articles (and poems) from a spiritual perspective, with an emphasis on the experiential, often related to language, Anthroposophy, Rosicrucianism, esoteric Christianity, Sophiology, and the Divine Feminine. His goal is to create a body of writing that is initiatory—that allows readers to grow beyond themselves.

Lucinda M. Vardey is the author/editor of nine books among them an anthology of women's prayers called *The Flowering of the Soul*, and *Mother Teresa: A*

Simple Path. After a decade of guiding pilgrimages and retreats in Tuscany, she began a lay community of women contemplatives now recognized by the Archdiocese of Toronto. In response to Pope Francis's invitation for a profound theology of women, she also founded the Magdala Conciliary on Feminine Theology, hosted a three-year seminar series on what is intrinsic to feminine theology in Rome between 2016-2018 and formed a Round Table on the Feminine Dimension of the Church also in Rome. She is currently editor of a new online journal, *With One Accord: Learning and Living the Feminine Dimension as Church* (www.magdalacolloquy.org). Her writing on contemplation and her blog Contemplating Jesus can be found on dallaluce.com.

Catrin Welz-Stein studied graphic design in Germany and worked as a graphic designer for various agencies.

In her spare time she experimented with mixed media, collages, and paintings on canvas and finally entered the amazing world of digital art. There she also discovered her passion and love of surrealism. Since then, her drive to create has never let go.

James Wetmore established the publishing company Sophia Perennis in 1995. He serves as co-director of Angelico Press, and produces the present journal. He has occupied himself for decades with the study, translation, and publishing of the writings of Valentin Tomberg.

Thomas Whittier is a gardener and landscape designer as well as a Third Order Carmelite. He is currently working on a manuscript, *Carols of Solitude*. He lives on the west coast of Ireland.